"Part memoir, part leadership guide,
Win-Win Deal Making *models good negotiation practices
alongside an intriguing overview of global affairs."*
—Foreword Clarion Reviews

WIN-WIN
DEAL MAKING

One Printers Way
Altona, MB R0G 0B0
Canada

www.friesenpress.com

Copyright © 2024 by Erik Richer La Flèche
First Edition — 2024

All rights reserved.

No part of this publication may be reproduced in any form, or by any means, electronic or mechanical, including photocopying, recording, or any information browsing, storage, or retrieval system, without permission in writing from FriesenPress.

ISBN
978-1-03-832452-8 (Hardcover)
978-1-03-832451-1 (Paperback)
978-1-03-832453-5 (eBook)

1. BUSINESS & ECONOMICS, NEGOTIATING

Distributed to the trade by The Ingram Book Company

WIN-WIN DEAL MAKING

LESSONS FROM THE ROAD

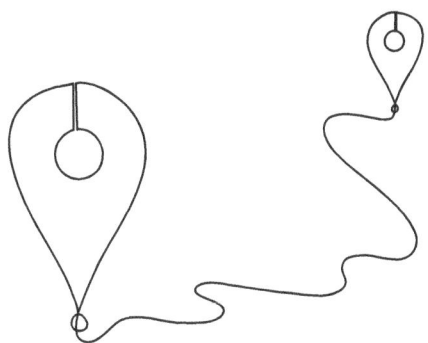

ERIK RICHER LA FLÈCHE

To Carolina, with love and gratitude.

TABLE OF CONTENTS

INTRODUCTION 1

CH 1.   SHOWING UP. 9

CH 2.   SUCCINCT AND TO THE POINT 23

CH 3.   IDENTIFICATION, ALLOCATION, MITIGATION. 37

CH 4.   STABILITY AND PREDICTABILITY 51

CH 5.   COMMON OBJECTIVES 69

CH 6.   OPPORTUNITY. 91

CH 7.   SHARING. 105

CH 8.   ALL POLITICS IS LOCAL 115

CH 9.   GREAT GAME 123

CH 10. INDIA 129

CH 11. POWER OF THE BRAND. 139

CH 12. LOCAL KNOWLEDGE, ARTIFICIAL INTELLIGENCE . .147

CONCLUSION. 151

APPENDIX I 155

APPENDIX II 175

GLOSSARY OF ABBREVIATIONS. 189

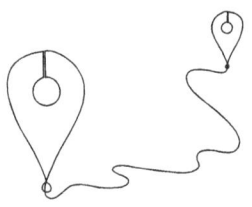

INTRODUCTION

"Luck is what happens when preparation meets opportunity."
—Seneca the Younger

The quote above is attributed to the first-century Roman philosopher and statesman Seneca the Younger and best describes my professional journey. Like many, I have spent much time preparing and far less time planning. Serendipity has played a large role in the development of my legal career. As a lawyer, I crossed paths with many opportunities and, with hindsight, realize that I only identified a fraction of them and seized even fewer. Nonetheless, the few that I did embrace provided me with an unusual and rewarding professional and personal journey.

Since 1979, I have negotiated transactions and otherwise rendered legal services in more than forty countries and autonomous territories. In the last two decades, as improvements in telecommunications and computing greatly reduced the need to leave Canada and be present in-country, I have worked remotely on transactions with a further twenty-five or so jurisdictions. Much of the work has involved large-scale projects centred around infrastructure, natural resources, and heavy industry. The projects rarely involved Canadian interests, whether private or public. When abroad, the clients were foreign governments, corporations, and entrepreneurs.

Thanks to my practice, I have had a front-row seat to learning and comparing how different countries, political systems, and cultures carry out projects and handle commercial and non-commercial risks. I have had a lot of fun and many adventures. Some will say that I was lucky. I agree, but I would add that I was also willing, curious, a little naive, and very stubborn.

This book is not a biography or a travelogue. I have merely tried to distill lessons from my years spent around the globe and provide context as to how I came to such lessons. I wrote the book in the hope that some of what I learned may be useful to others. I hasten to add that what I learned falls in the commonsense and first-principles categories and is definitively not "rocket science." Most lessons are widely known, often intuitively, yet it is truly remarkable how often they are forgotten or ignored due to time and other pressures. Hopefully, my experiences will buttress resistance to such pressures if only because giving way usually comes at a cost, financial or otherwise. The lessons I learned are apposite to all jurisdictions, whether a member of the G7 or the Global South.

As a legal professional, I am subject to confidentiality obligations. Only parties and details clearly in the public domain have been expressly identified, and even then, only in a circumscribed manner. When unable to refer to

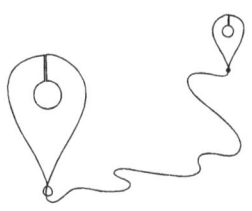

INTRODUCTION

> *"Luck is what happens when preparation meets opportunity."*
> —Seneca the Younger

The quote above is attributed to the first-century Roman philosopher and statesman Seneca the Younger and best describes my professional journey. Like many, I have spent much time preparing and far less time planning. Serendipity has played a large role in the development of my legal career. As a lawyer, I crossed paths with many opportunities and, with hindsight, realize that I only identified a fraction of them and seized even fewer. Nonetheless, the few that I did embrace provided me with an unusual and rewarding professional and personal journey.

Since 1979, I have negotiated transactions and otherwise rendered legal services in more than forty countries and autonomous territories. In the last two decades, as improvements in telecommunications and computing greatly reduced the need to leave Canada and be present in-country, I have worked remotely on transactions with a further twenty-five or so jurisdictions. Much of the work has involved large-scale projects centred around infrastructure, natural resources, and heavy industry. The projects rarely involved Canadian interests, whether private or public. When abroad, the clients were foreign governments, corporations, and entrepreneurs.

Thanks to my practice, I have had a front-row seat to learning and comparing how different countries, political systems, and cultures carry out projects and handle commercial and non-commercial risks. I have had a lot of fun and many adventures. Some will say that I was lucky. I agree, but I would add that I was also willing, curious, a little naive, and very stubborn.

This book is not a biography or a travelogue. I have merely tried to distill lessons from my years spent around the globe and provide context as to how I came to such lessons. I wrote the book in the hope that some of what I learned may be useful to others. I hasten to add that what I learned falls in the commonsense and first-principles categories and is definitively not "rocket science." Most lessons are widely known, often intuitively, yet it is truly remarkable how often they are forgotten or ignored due to time and other pressures. Hopefully, my experiences will buttress resistance to such pressures if only because giving way usually comes at a cost, financial or otherwise. The lessons I learned are apposite to all jurisdictions, whether a member of the G7 or the Global South.

As a legal professional, I am subject to confidentiality obligations. Only parties and details clearly in the public domain have been expressly identified, and even then, only in a circumscribed manner. When unable to refer to specific instances or details, I have regrouped my experiences and expressed myself in generic terms.

I am fortunate to have been able to carry on with my sometimes-unorthodox practice from three very mainstream corporate law firms: Courtois, Clarkson, Parsons and Tétrault (CCPT) (now the Montreal office of McCarthy Tétrault); Anderson Mōri & Tomotsune (Tokyo) (formerly Anderson Mōri & Rabinowitz); and Stikeman Elliott (SE). I owe each firm a great deal, and I thank them wholeheartedly. The first gave me the opportunity to become a lawyer and then seconded me to Japan where I lived for more than four years. The second exposed me to new countries and novel ways of doing things. The third gave me the time and means to ply my trade in Canada and abroad for more than three decades.

Throughout much of my career, I was the unwitting and fortunate beneficiary of three secular trends:

GLOBALIZATION. In the second half of the twentieth century, and especially from the late 1970s, new international trade agreements and improvements in logistics and telecommunications made it much easier for businesses to open new markets, incorporate new locales into their supply chains, and, as was the case with clothing and other labour-intensive sectors, relocate entire industries to less expensive and regulated jurisdictions. This trend engendered a veritable rush to invest in lesser-developed countries—nowhere more so than in Asia. Globalization was one of the forces that allowed China to become "the world's factory" by the end of the last century.

EXPANSION OF THE RULE OF LAW. In the mid-1980s, the World Bank and other international financial institutions (IFIs) came to the realization that "regime change" was likely to occur in many countries, whether they were members of the Soviet bloc or former colonies of the West. A solid legal foundation would then be necessary if these countries were to attract foreign investment and become successful democracies with open market economies. In order to assist these jurisdictions in their transition, the IFIs made funding available to secure technical assistance from foreign and domestic jurists, all with a view to introducing the rule of law as commonly understood in Western democracies.

PRIVATIZATION. By the end of the 1980s, many jurisdictions had become disillusioned with the performance of state-owned enterprises (SOEs) and government agencies and decided to embark on wide-scale privatizations with the objective of increasing efficiency and innovation, reducing the burden on state treasuries, and making better use of finite government resources. The United Kingdom under Prime Minister Margaret Thatcher was a pathbreaker in this regard. It led a wave of privatizations around the world that crested in the 1990s, but continues today in one form or another, including the provision of government services and infrastructure through public-private partnerships (PPPs) and concessions.

I did not fully recognize these trends, at first, and so I rode them like a cork on water. A very imperfect ability to discern trends and opportunities only came much later in my career and was the fruit of experience rather than keen analytical skill. After being accepted dogma for more than forty years, the three trends described above are now being reconsidered in much of the world.

The COVID-19 pandemic laid bare the shortcomings of unfettered globalization. Governments of all stripes now want to move productive capacity back to their shores, or at least closer to their borders, so that they are not at the mercy of uncertain supply chains for their basic needs. This trend reversal has provided wordsmiths with an opportunity to produce a colourful suite of words to describe the new approach: "On shoring," "near shoring," and "friend shoring" are but a few examples of their work product. Environmental and armed challenges to shipping in recent years—whether it be the low water levels of the Panama Canal, piracy from the shores of the Horn of Africa, or missile attacks from insurgents in Yemen—are also eroding the case for globalization.

At the same time, many governments and their electorates have reduced their appetite for private-sector solutions and laissez-faire policies. Big government or, at the very least, dirigiste government, is back in vogue. Such change of policy is grounded in domestic politics and feeds on voter anxieties caused by slower economic growth, stagnant wages, higher inflation, increasing public deficits, the rationing of public services, growing wealth disparity, and other ills, real or perceived.

But, perhaps, the most consequential new trend is the desire of many countries to challenge the rules-based order that has prevailed since the end of the Second World War. From my experience, many in the Global South view the current rules as favouring the West at the expense of the Global South. This challenge to the West in international affairs is often accompanied domestically with attacks on the rule of law and the freedoms that flow from it.

Authoritarians and populists on all continents are finding a sympathetic ear with populations that are disabused and impatient with traditional politicians and bureaucrats and their complex, nuanced, and slow-acting solutions to problems. The fact that many solutions proffered by experts are less than effective, often because of corruption and other bad behaviour, only corrodes further the trust they may have once had in their governments.

Over the course of my practice, I have had the good fortune to meet and learn from hundreds, and although I remember only a few by name, I am grateful to all of them for generously and candidly sharing their knowledge and observations. Sometimes the shortest conversations were the most memorable.

In Benin in the mid-1990s, I struck up a light conversation at the airport with a German engineer while we were waiting to board our plane. Birds were flying happily in the airport terminal. After observing them, he remarked with a sardonic smile that the "difference between the First World and the Third World was maintenance." The phrase is reductionist and unfair. Developed country politicians, like their brethren elsewhere, much prefer inaugurating new constructions than funding maintenance and renovations. This having been said, I have often repeated the phrase with considerable effect. I use it when discussing maintenance obligations with government officials in the hope of getting them to increase maintenance budgets and, by extension, the useful life of infrastructure. Remarkably, the German engineer's phrase has helped me achieve the desired result more often than not.

As with most endeavours, little of what I have done would have been possible without the help and work of many. In addition to the few mentioned later in this book, I would like to especially recognize a small number of lawyers who were instrumental at one time or another in my practice and who themselves have much to share: Noritaka Moriuchi, Tamostu Hatasawa, Alain Massicotte, Martin Scheim, Christine Desaulniers, Raj Kumar Dubey, and Carlos Larrain.

The lessons summarized in this book were gleaned primarily from the many long-duration projects I had the good fortune to work on. But the lessons are equally apposite to all manner of transactions, whether big or small, or of short or long duration.

I have worked on many types of transactions in diverse industries. One of the reasons I was able to do this and quickly adapt to market conditions — or "reinvent" myself as some would observe — was the realization early on that, at their core, all transactions have similar features. What is important is to identify the transaction's risks, allocate such risks to the parties best able to manage them, and mitigate the consequences of each risk should it materialize.

Montreal, Canada, May 2024

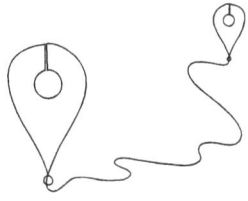

CHAPTER ONE

SHOWING UP

In the fall of 1973, I applied to McGill University's Faculty of Law. I was in my last year of high school at Collège Stanislas in Montreal. Stanislas, or Stan as it is commonly known, is a kindergarten through Grade 12 French curriculum school founded in 1938 and financially supported by the governments of France and Quebec. Valéry Giscard d'Estaing, the president of France from 1974 to 1981, taught there in 1947. It is one of more than five hundred establishments that form part of the French school system abroad. In 2023, the system had more than 370,000 students in 139 countries.

I chose to study law because I had not yet decided on a career path and believed that law would make a perfect perch from which to decide my professional future. In doing so I was simply following the popular French adage: *"Le droit mène à tout à condition d'en sortir"* (law leads to everything provided that you leave it). I learned only much, much later that the phrase is most often attributed to Henri Queuille, a French twentieth century politician known for his wit and sometimes bitting sense of humour.

I chose McGill because it was convenient. I lived five hundred metres from the law school. My extended family was familiar with the university. Two decades earlier, an aunt and an uncle had graduated from the law school. Another uncle was an alumnus of the medical faculty.

My McGill application was the only university application I would ever complete. The thought of hedging my bet by applying to other programs or universities never crossed my mind until well after the deadlines for such applications had come and gone and I was anxiously waiting for word from McGill. I was greatly relieved when I received my late acceptance. I got the good news while living on a schooner in Nova Scotia. It was a beautiful summer day. A fitting start to my budding legal career.

After obtaining two law degrees from McGill (BCL 1977, LLB 1978), I passed my Quebec Bar exams and successfully articled at Courtois, Clarkson, Parsons and Tétrault, arguably Montreal's most blue-blooded corporate firm at the time. And in 1979, I commenced work as an associate, earning C$16,500 a year.

Law in Canada in the 1970s was still a local affair. Law firms, with few exceptions, had only one office and practised the law of a single jurisdiction. There were many regulatory barriers to multi-office firms — not to say anything about multi-jurisdiction firms. Moreover, the profession was tradition-bound. Change came slowly. When you joined an established firm as an associate, you were expected to remain until you made partner or were told otherwise. As a partner, you generally stayed put until retirement. If a partner left, it was to become a judge, enter politics, or, somewhat less desirably, become in-house counsel with a large corporation. Any departure from this model was unusual and could cast a shadow on the partner's character. It was a bit like how divorce in those days could disqualify a man from high public office or the presidency of a major bank or publicly listed corporation. While mobility was limited, it did create a relatively collegial atmosphere. Firms were smaller and imprinted with the character and foibles of their senior partners. Today's major law firms are larger, more diverse, and far better managed, but they seem to have less personality and the differences among them are less pronounced despite the best efforts of their marketing departments.

While a few firms were establishing representative offices abroad in the late 1970s, such as CCPT in Brussels and SE in London, foreign contacts and networks were the primary source of inbound work. It is with this in mind that Jacques Courtois, the managing partner of CCPT, would travel around the world weaving a network of "best friends" and correspondent law firms.

Unlike today, the profession at the time was less concerned with conflicts of interest. Senior lawyers could wear many hats. Courtois was no exception: lawyer, bank director, major political fundraiser, and, last but not least, president of the Montreal Canadiens hockey team — at the time, the most storied professional ice hockey team in the world. From 1950 to 1980, the Canadiens won the Stanley Cup sixteen times, professional hockey's highest honour.

Japan in the early 1980s was what China was in the '00s: fast growing, rapidly modernizing, optimistic, ambitious, and starting to invest abroad. Japan's nominal GDP surpassed West Germany's in 1968, making it the second largest economy in the world after the US. By 1980, Japan's economic rise had made Japan a lightning rod for US criticism of its export-led growth model and its numerous disingenuous non-tariff barriers. After four decades of being in the crosshairs of the US, Japan was more than happy to pass that torch to China in 2010 when the latter overtook Japan as the world's second largest economy. Much of the economic criticism heaped on China today resonates with what the US and Europe said about Japan in the 1980s.

The state of Japan in 1980 was in sharp contrast with what was going on in North America: inflation combined with low economic growth and high unemployment, rising trade deficits, rusting and uncompetitive manufacturing sectors, the Iran hostage crisis, and high interest rates. The US prime rate hit a high of 21.5 percent on December 19, 1980, and would remain at double digits until 1985.

On a more local level, in 1980, Quebec held the first of two independence referenda — the second one was in 1995. Although the first referendum was won 3 to 2 by the remain-in-Canada side, the exodus of head offices and their English-speaking employees from Quebec — which had started in the early 1970s — continued unabated.

It is against this background that Courtois decided, in 1980, to add Tokyo to his regular tours. One of the obligatory stops in Tokyo was the law firm of Anderson Mōri & Rabinowitz (AMR). In 2005, AMR merged with another firm to become Anderson Mōri & Tomotsune, one of the current "Big Four" Japanese law firms.

At the time of Courtois's visit, AMR was headed by larger-than-life Richard W. Rabinowitz, an American who during the Second World War, and after fighting with US forces in North Africa, was transferred back to the US for Japanese language training. After the war, he attended Yale and Harvard and in 1953 registered as a "quasi member" of the Japanese Bar—an oddly named membership category open to foreign qualified attorneys. This separate category was abolished in 1955.

AMR was founded in 1963. In 1980, it had grown to approximately forty lawyers: thirty Japanese and ten "foreign legal apprentices" (FLAs). FLAs were young, foreign qualified attorneys who had no recognized professional status in Japan but could get a working visa as an "apprentice." At AMR, the FLAs had a number of very precise tasks.

The first task of FLAs was to facilitate communication, both oral and written, between AMR and its clients. AMR was a Japanese-English bilingual firm with English being the preferred language of communication with clients, as most of the firm's clients were English-speaking or were involved in international transactions where the common language was English. English was widely taught in Japanese high schools, but mastered by few. Japanese English teachers were generally proficient with reading and writing, but speaking was a different affair with many unable to hold a conversation. This state of affairs has changed little, and as a result, there exists to this day in Japan, as elsewhere in East Asia, a strong demand for native English speakers to teach English as a second language. These courses help high school and university students, as well as office and other workers, be conversant for study or work.

The second task of FLAs was to quickly become familiar with the basic tenets of Japanese law so as to be useful in the preparation of legal memoranda and opinions and the negotiation and drafting of contracts. AMR's library had a large selection of English translations of Japanese laws. These were either commercially available or prepared in-house. The library also had a compilation of relevant AMR legal memoranda and opinions. The Japanese legal system is a civilian system whose civil and commercial codes were heavily inspired by the laws of Germany and, to a lesser extent, France. This extensive legal codification greatly assisted the FLAs in acquiring a useful understanding of basic principles of Japanese contract and commercial law.

Japanese associates at major Japanese firms were expected, after a few years of practice, to move to an English-speaking country — usually the US — and complete a Master of Law as a way to perfect their language skills and become better acculturated with Western societies. The Japanese associates would also spend some time in a large foreign firm to better understand their inner workings and develop their networks. The Japanese firms generally provided these associates with financial and other assistance, and upon completion of their stint abroad, the associates would return to the sponsoring firms.

The third task of FLAs was to assist these lawyers to improve their English language skills and otherwise prepare for their stay abroad.

Except for a couple of grandfathered law firms, 1980 Japan was closed to foreign law firms. Within the shielded Japanese market, AMR was a powerhouse. It was, despite its small size by Anglo-American standards, one of the largest law firms in Japan. Moreover, its client roster was unsurpassed. AMR represented a plurality of the Fortune 500 doing business in Japan, as well as many foreign banks. It also assisted Japanese corporations in investing in Asia and beyond. FLAs were mostly Americans with the occasional Brit or Aussie. No Canadian had ever been an FLA at AMR or, to my knowledge, at any other firm.

Courtois and Rabinowitz hit it off immediately. Rabinowitz was born in New Haven, Connecticut, and had been a high school hockey goaltender. As an adult, he remained a passionate student of the game. Rabinowitz was fond of saying that "lawyering was not a sometimes thing" and was very dedicated to his busy practice. Yet, he often arranged his agenda so he could attend games of the six-team Japan Ice Hockey League, a rather obscure corporation-sponsored organization that passed as the senior hockey league in Japan. It was disbanded in 2004 and replaced by another no less obscure hockey league with teams in Japan and South Korea. Each hockey team was composed of Japanese employees of the sponsoring corporation with one or two ringers, usually Canadian but sometimes American or from the USSR. To say that Rabinowitz was thrilled to become acquainted with the president of the world's most prestigious hockey team would be a gross understatement. After much talk about hockey in Rabinowitz's spacious and comfortable corner office in the AIU building overlooking the outer moat of the Imperial Palace in central Tokyo, it was settled: The next FLA would be a Canadian and come from CCPT. Rabinowitz's love of hockey was genuine and deep. When Ken Dryden, the Montreal Canadiens' star goaltender and McGill law graduate, published his book *The Game* in 1983, Rabinowitz gave me a copy declaring it one of the best books ever written about sports.

Upon his return to Montreal, Courtois requested CVs from six single, male corporate law associates and sent them to Tokyo. After a little to-and-fro, I was selected and offered a three-year secondment at what I would come to believe was the most prestigious law firm in the brightest economy in the world. Moving to Japan seemed a no-brainer. But mine was a minority view, and many well-thinking individuals felt the need to advise that I was going against convention and irreparably scuttling my career.

I was not convinced by this gloomy advice, but made up my mind only after I was approached by a headhunter who also happened to be the father of a high school classmate. He was tasked with finding a suitable junior lawyer to join the in-house legal team of a German multinational. After a few years of training in Germany, I would be sent back to Canada. I was flattered, but having spent half my childhood in France and having studied German for five years in high school, the idea of living and working in a highly structured European country just did not have the same appeal as being a *gaijin* in Japan.

Japan was and remains a tradition-bound and somewhat stifling culture for the Japanese and those trying to integrate, the latter being a lost cause for many. But for the temporary resident, it can be a relatively free space as there are few expectations of conformity. On the other hand, the German proposition, while unexciting, did have the advantage of confirming that the legal profession could accommodate lawyers with a more international inclination.

So I accepted AMR's offer and arrived in Tokyo in 1981 eager to explore and learn. I was twenty-five and having an adventure. Tokyo is an expensive city, but my salary of 6.6 million yen plus bonus would more than adequately cover my expenses and generate sufficient disposable income to discover Japan and explore Asia. Remarkably, because of the low inflation in Japan over the last four decades, my 1981 salary would still provide me with a somewhat comfortable wage in 2024. Each time I visit Japan, I am surprised by how prices have remained similar to those I knew when first there. This is obviously not the case in North America or Europe, to say nothing of most emerging markets.

Within days of my arrival, I rented a small apartment in Hiroo not far from Arisugawa garden. It was next to the

Finnish embassy and two hundred metres from a complex housing personnel from the embassy of the People's Republic of China. Because of my neighbours, there was a *koban* close to my building. A *koban* is a small police outpost found throughout Japan in metropolitan areas. Whenever someone important was visiting my neighbourhood, a policeman in Samurai-like riot gear would be stationed at the base of my building. My neighbourhood police never asked me to show my passport or *Gaikokujin Tōroku Shōmeisho*, the alien registration booklet issued by one's municipality that had to be carried at all times, but it was evident that they knew who I was. Sometimes they would jokingly call out my name when I passed in front of them while returning from a late night in neighbouring Roppongi, one of Tokyo's entertainment districts. In 2012, the municipal registration system was replaced by a national system.

The work at AMR was primarily transactional and regulatory. The bulk of the clientele was American, and for reasons of cultural affinity, the American FLAs in tandem with Japanese attorneys handled American clients. This work was Tokyo-based and sedentary. Being a dual Canadian and French national, I was assigned to non-US clients, primarily Japanese with the odd European bank or multinational. With the notable exception of Nortel—Canada's undisputed technology champion at the time—Canadian corporations in those days had a very low profile in Japan and were for all practical purposes absent from AMR's client roster. For Japanese clients, the work consisted of representing their interests in transactions in Asia, the Middle East, and North Africa. That meant that I would often have to travel and work outside Japan, and so I very quickly began to spend a fair bit of time in Indonesia and South Korea.

My work rarely involved North America or Europe as the Japanese were more than ably represented there. Only in very time-sensitive matters would I be involved with these regions, usually playing the role of glorified courier between Tokyo and New York or London. There was one period in particular when I spent a lot of time in planes because the all-powerful Ministry of International Trade and Industry (MITI) had issued "guidance" that Japanese leasing and trading companies should purchase Boeing and McDonnell Douglas aircrafts, US-built oil rigs, and other large items to lease back to US companies. The primary purpose of these transactions was to reduce trade frictions between Japan and the US. Assets so purchased could be counted as exports to Japan, despite never leaving the US or its airspace and territorial waters.

Japan was continuously on the lookout for stratagems to improve the optics, if not the reality, of its unbalanced commercial relationship with the US. Some of the stratagems employed by Japan were laughably simple. One of my favourites involved Japan booking for statistical purposes exports to the US on an FOB basis. This meant that the price of the exports did not include costs, insurance, and freight. The value of imports from the US, meanwhile, was calculated on a CIF basis where the price did include such additional items, thus inflating the price of imports and deflating the price of exports.

MITI was created in 1949 and merged in 2001 with other agencies to form the Ministry of Economy, Trade, and Industry (METI). MITI was an essential pillar of the "Japanese economic miracle" of the 1960s and was replicated in much of Asia in some form or another, including by the "Four Asian Tigers": Taiwan, Singapore, Hong Kong, and South Korea. MITI was at its most powerful when it guided Japan through two periods: import substitution (1950s and 1960s) and export-focused growth (1970s and early 1980s). During that period, MITI allocated financial and other resources among Japanese companies and imposed import and export constraints. For example, from 1981 to 1994, Japanese car manufacturers under the guidance of MITI "voluntarily" agreed to limit the number of Japanese cars exported to the US. This had the effect of artificially increasing the price of Japanese cars in the US, thus giving US manufacturers greater pricing power and time to reorganize and improve. The ministry lost a lot of influence in the 1990s with the growing maturity of the Japanese corporate world and the creation of the World Trade Organization (WTO) in 1995.

As China and many others in Asia—most notably India, Indonesia, and Vietnam—continue to expand their manufacturing capacities, there is a very real possibility that the G7 and other developed economies will have to resort again to import controls similar to those mentioned above. Should productive capacity in Asia greatly exceed the needs of their domestic markets or should Asian manufacturers produce quality products at much lower prices, they will want to export. Trade frictions will then ensue.

The car industry, as it moves away from the internal combustion engine, is likely to require protection in both North America and Europe. The same may be true for other industries, such as PV panels and batteries. The preferred import control method is tariffs, but these may not be sufficient if consumers—notwithstanding high prices—opt for Asian-made products with superior features and quality. This is history repeating itself, except that this time, the G7 and the West generally are heavily indebted, have reduced industrial capacity, and do not have political and economic hegemony.

Thinking about it now, it is somewhat surprising that hockey had such a central role in my professional career. I never played organized hockey growing up. I was a skier with only a tangential interest in hockey as a spectator sport. But without hockey, I probably would have never moved to Tokyo. I would have experienced Asia as a tourist and had a more traditional North American or transatlantic legal career.

This would be the first of several moments when I benefited from something that had little to do with my qualifications or interests. To paraphrase a former managing partner of SE, success more often than not requires just showing up. In this instance, it was more a case of being at the right place at the right time. A sort of "being there" moment like in the 1971 novel of the same name and the 1979 movie starring Peter Sellers. All I had to do after showing up was seize the moment.

Of course, an opportunity is often withdrawn or fails to materialize before you can seize it; in that case, all you can do is quickly forget about the matter and move on. After Japan, the majority of my foreign work was obtained through calls for tenders and calls for proposals. Participating in competitive processes, whether in sport or business, is a great way to develop resiliency as you quickly learn that you do not always win and that it is not always clear why you fail — the latter thought leading me greatly to privilege opportunities that afforded some degree of control over the outcome.

In 1998, I was asked by the Canadian government if I was interested in becoming the general counsel of the Asian Development Bank (ADB) based in Manila. The ADB is a regional IFI traditionally headed by a Japanese national. This is similar to the way the World Bank is customarily led by an American or the International Monetary Fund by a European. The other senior posts at these institutions are distributed amongst the bank's major shareholders according to an informal understanding among them.

I was told at the time that the general counsel position at the ADB was reserved for Americans. But because the US was interested in nominating someone in another institution for a post ordinarily attributed to a Canadian, the US was offering Canada the post of general counsel of the ADB in exchange. After consulting with my spouse, Carolina Gallo, I accepted Canada's gracious offer. Carolina and I had some familiarity with the Philippines, and we thought that it would be an interesting family adventure for us and our three young children.

I was quickly contacted by someone at External Affairs Canada (now Global Affairs Canada) whose sole task was to assist with the more prosaic aspects of moving Canadian candidacies forward at international organizations. The only comment from the all-important Japanese ADB shareholder was that, at forty-two, I might be a little young but otherwise there was no concern with my candidacy. So, after a few weeks of positive exchanges with Ottawa and Manila, the opportunity no longer appeared inchoate, and I started taking concrete steps regarding an eventual move. Then, late one evening—while I was with Carolina at the Lake Palace Hotel in Udaipur, India, the island palace of James Bond Octopussy fame — I got a phone call from Ottawa. My handler very matter-of-factly advised me that the post of general counsel of the ADB was no longer being offered to Canada, the US having decided to retain it. My handler then quickly thanked me and hung up. In seconds, the opportunity of a lifetime disappeared. I was disappointed, but less for having lost the opportunity and more for the complete lack of control I had over the process. I resolved at that moment that I would continue to "show up," but would privilege opportunities where I had some degree of control over the outcome.

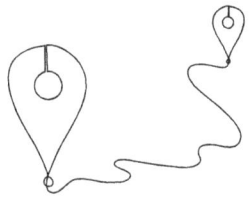

CHAPTER TWO

SUCCINCT AND TO THE POINT

THE TELEX

When I arrived at AMR in 1981, the office was modern and well equipped by the standards of the day. It used boxy, early generation word processors with green screens, noisy printers that produced one page a minute, bulky and slow photocopiers, land line phones that rang incessantly, fax machines that could only communicate with a few compatible machines, and, last but not least, the venerable telex. There was, of course, no mobile telephony, portable computer, or internet.

The telex, supplanted in the mid- to late 1980s by the fax machine, itself now displaced by email in most businesses and governments, had been around since the 1930s and may be best described as a network of station-to-station machines capable of sending telegraph-like messages using telephone wires.

The telex had two main advantages at AMR. When communicating with North America and Europe, it was an easy way to bridge time differences yet quickly correspond on a cost-effective manner. International telephony from Japan was expensive, and fax machines were slow and somewhat clumsy to use. With much of Asia and beyond, it was a way to overcome imperfect telephone infrastructure. A telex message would usually get through even if the phone lines were congested or of poor quality. The same was not true of phone calls or faxes.

At AMR, I used the telex daily, and it quickly influenced how I came to approach transactions and draft legal documents. A telex message is essentially a telegram. Conciseness is therefore essential. Writing with concision saves time for the reader. In turn, that facilitates comprehension and, hopefully, results in a speedier meeting of the minds between the parties. It does, however, require more time and forethought on the part of the writer. French students from their earliest high school days learn about prolific writers, such as Madame de Pompadour and Blaise Pascal, who apologized to their correspondents for the length of their letters on account of not having the time to write shorter ones.

The telex also levelled the playing field between native and non-native English speakers. Content trumped form. The ability to write nice prose was less of an advantage. As a non-native English speaker, I found this to be most helpful.

CENTRAL MESSAGE

Although being succinct is no guarantee of clarity or accuracy, it does oblige the writer to concentrate on the central message to the exclusion of much else.

In the fall of 1974, I was fortunate to take the Obligations course with Professor Paul-André Crépeau. He was a Canadian civil law giant born in Saskatchewan, who, among his many accomplishments, headed with success the effort to modernize Quebec's Civil Code. Obligations was a foundational year-long course for all civil law students. Crépeau began his first lecture by emphasizing the importance of always being able to quickly and succinctly answer the phrase *"De quoi s'agit-il?"* (What is it about?) I was more than a little surprised that this phrase from my middle school days would underpin one of my first university classes, but I was also reassured because it validated a basic tenet of my education.

Over the years, when negotiating, I have had to retreat time and time again to ask, *De quoi s'agit-il?* This was never more effective than in one instance in India. It was the late 1990s, and we had been hired pursuant to a competitive process to assist the state electricity board (SEB) of a large southern Indian state. An Indian SEB is a state-owned enterprise that produces, transports, and distributes electricity within a state.

A well-known private Indian corporation, a household name in fact, wanted to build a very large thermal power plant and fuel port terminal and sell all the electricity generated by the plant to our client. The project was to be project financed; that is to say, the project's lenders would first look to the project's revenues in order to be repaid. Since the SEB was the project's sole client, the project's bankability rested on the financial capacity of the SEB to meet its obligations. We were brought in to help the SEB enhance its financial capacity and close the deal.

Upon arriving at the client's head office for the first time, I was immediately ushered into a very large room. On one side were the representatives of the Indian corporation, its two main international banks, and their US and Indian lawyers—about twelve people. The project's financing was large by any objective standard and had a sizeable US dollar tranche. On the other side were the representatives of the client—about forty in total, many sitting on what appeared to be a bleacher. No one had briefed me nor wanted to take the time to do so. As a result, I had only a rather cursory understanding as to the status of the mandate.

After the usual polite entreaties, the US lawyers listed the draft agreements that they had sent over to our client and asked whether we had any queries or comments. I had not been provided with a copy of the drafts, and I was unsure whether they had been analyzed by our client, so I informed the other side. Needless to say, the other side was most unimpressed and let us have it for the next fifteen or so minutes. Once they had stopped, I rose and went to a whiteboard that was located between the two sides and asked our client's representatives, all forty of them, whether anyone could summarize the salient features of the transaction and the risks associated with it. A cacophony ensued, and after ten minutes, it was obvious to all concerned that a little regrouping was in order and that we would all have to step back, remind everyone of the objectives of the transaction, and move sequentially at a deliberate pace. There was no other way, notwithstanding that the parties had been negotiating on and off for nine years!

MUST-HAVE POINTS

Ordinarily, businesses used the telex to send straightforward messages, such as purchase orders and delivery date confirmations. But AMR's telex messages habitually dealt with more complicated matters. Telexes, in the early stages of transactions, would, in addition to the central message, include the client's "must-have" points as well as try to anticipate and answer those questions most likely to be asked by the reader.

Like many lawyers, I try early on to get the client to identify their must-have points. I use a three-bucket approach—must-have points, good-to-have points, and nice-to-have points—and introduce them into the negotiations sequentially, starting with the must-have points. In a nutshell, must-have points are the critical elements without which there can be no transaction—the so-called deal breakers. Each transaction only has a few such points, and it is imperative for the credibility of each side that their classification be true. There is little to gain, and much to lose, by misclassifying lesser issues as must-have points—an error many lawyers make at the beginning of their careers.

Good-to-have points are secondary matters that flesh out and complement must-have points. Nice-to-have points are elements, often procedural, that are helpful but not essential in carrying out the transaction. Nice-to-have provisions include, for example, clauses that facilitate interpretation or the management of the contractual relationship, such as notification procedures.

Whether a point is good-to-have or nice-to-have, and whether it must be included in a contract, will sometimes depend on the governing law. Contracts in a jurisdiction with developed civil and other codes tend to be shorter than in other jurisdictions. The codification of contractual and other basic legal principles affords a measure of certainty that is not always present in other legal systems. As a result, lawyers in civilian jurisdictions are more likely to leave out of contracts well-established principles of general law that are clearly set out elsewhere. This results in contracts that are shorter and easier to read and understand.

TRANSACTION DOCUMENTATION

It is my experience that most complex transactions have been through at least two discrete sets of documents before the parties sign the third and final set. Note that each set of documents may itself be the product of several, if not numerous, iterations. At first, the parties enter into a letter of intent or short form memorandum of understanding or agreement whereby they set out the broad outlines of the transaction, the must-have points, and how the parties will proceed with their due diligence and further negotiations.

The second set is more fulsome. In addition to repeating and amplifying upon what is provided in the first set of documentation, the second set will add the good-to-have points, consider the result of the due diligence carried out to date, and seek to mitigate transaction risks that have been identified.

The third and final set of documents will build upon the second set and include many of the so-called nice-to-have provisions. At AMR, the telex was generally used only for the first set of documents.

A sequential approach serves several purposes:

1. The first set of documents provides a clear statement of the main aspects of the transaction. This, among other things, allows the parties to quickly refresh their memories as to the ambit of the transaction and limits the opportunity for transaction creep or drift.

2. A sequential approach prevents negotiators from burdening the transaction with a lot of items of lesser importance before properly dealing with items of greater importance. Some negotiators proceed pell-mell and without care as to the relative importance of various points. In transactions under time constraints, this may result in issues of significant importance not being given the attention they deserve because precious time was devoted to the examination of minor matters.

    Not all contractual provisions are of equal weight. Failing to deal with essential matters first will likely cause friction later in the negotiations and delay the transaction. Such friction and delay can derail or sink a transaction. This is particularly true when one or more of the parties is a large corporation, a government, or a SOE. When dealing with large bureaucracies, it is difficult—once the basic terms and conditions of a transaction have been approved by such bureaucracy and its highest bodies, such as a council of ministers or a board of directors—to go back and ask for changes. This can be done perhaps once or twice, but by the third time, the loss of confidence in the negotiators and the resistance to further change is too great and the request is likely to be denied.

3. As the transaction moves from letter of intent to heads of agreement to final agreements, the progression

helps build momentum toward a successful close as the points become easier to dispose of despite being more numerous.

COMMUNICATIONS

When I started travelling in Asia on behalf of AMR, I quickly became confronted with a number of constraints. I was usually the only AMR representative embedded with the client's negotiating team. Time differences, telecommunication costs, and poor infrastructure made communications with the Tokyo office somewhat difficult. Exchanges with the Japanese client's on-site team were often hindered by language and culture. Communications with the other side could be equally difficult, although in very large transactions, the other side was usually represented by US, English, or Hong Kong legal and financial advisers.

Access to reference materials other than what little I could bring with me in my suitcases was difficult. Paper is heavy, and weight limited the amount of material I could bring. Confidentiality is a serious concern in some jurisdictions, so mailing or couriering material was out of the question. Fax machines were slow and not always available. Computers were not yet portable and mobile telephony was the stuff of science fiction. I quickly came to the realization that I would need to develop a set of simple drafting and analytical tools that would allow me to function in environments less well-equipped than AMR's Tokyo office. And so, I proceeded to write down my observations on each trip and try to extract general rules that I could use on the road.

The first observation was obvious. I would have to change the way I expressed myself in English. I would have to learn to speak at a more deliberate pace. It could be faster than Voice of America's slow English language programs, but slower than normal English language radio programs. More importantly, I would have to learn to write simply and stick to words with plain and clear meaning—words that are easily searchable in a concise dictionary. As a result, I came to banish jargon and colloquialisms that are difficult to explain quickly. I also concluded that most people use jargon out of laziness so as to avoid having to make the effort to be precise. Finally, I avoided "weasel words," preferring to spell out and explain any concern I might have.

The second observation was that I had to find an efficient and consistent way to express my deal concerns. Risk is a concept that is widely used and understood by clients and their advisers, whether they be technical, financial, or legal. It quickly dawned on me that if I consistently expressed my concerns as risks in a language devoid of legalese, it was easier for everyone to understand my concerns and participate in the resolution of the issue.

Because most of the transactions on which I worked were long-duration transactions, as opposed to shorter ones, it was necessary not only to identify transaction risks but also to ensure that each party assuming a risk was able to do so and to mitigate consequences should the risk occur. A successful allocation of a risk in a long-duration transaction is very different than in a shorter transaction and takes greater forethought. "Buyer beware" has little place when dealing with a joint venture involving a multibillion-dollar refinery with a useful life of thirty years and more. The next chapter discusses risks more fully, including their allocation and mitigation.

The third observation was that the structure and presentation of written documents was very important. I learned to insert titles to guide the reader and divide text into many easily digestible paragraphs, each dealing with one subject and numbered for quick reference. Sentences were short and declarative, with the end of each sentence introducing the topic of the next sentence. I also tried to borrow as best I could from the way our Japanese clients presented material. They were less verbose and more visually effective. They made extensive use of matrices, tables, and graphs in their internal communications, and I tried to incorporate these in my work.

The fourth observation was that our Japanese clients were insistent on understanding and approving all the provisions of a contract and would quiz me at length regarding every contractual detail. Everything had to be explained and considered, often more than once. There was no delegation of negotiating authority to the lawyers irrespective of the relative importance of a clause. All clauses received the same treatment, from the essential ones to those considered boilerplate. The above usually was an intellectually painful exercise carried out at the end of the day and well into the night. As a result, I quickly learned whenever I had "the pen" to include in contracts only the essential elements.

GOOD FAITH

The Japanese clients generally tried to shun the highly precise and fulsome legalistic prose familiar to Anglo-American lawyers. Japanese contracts tended to be much shorter than North American ones, and they usually included a paragraph to the effect that the parties agreed to discuss in good faith any contractual lacuna. This "further assurances" clause made Western-trained lawyers anxious and exacerbated their proclivity for adding much language in their search for greater certainty.

Many of our Japanese clients were fond of saying that life is too complicated for a contract or a law to cover all eventualities. Although my Japanese interlocutors were generally in good faith, I have often heard the same reasoning applied disingenuously by governments looking for opportunities to avoid meeting their obligations.

In the 1990s and even the '00s it was still common for government officials, particularly in emerging markets, to state with a straight face that, notwithstanding the commercial nature of a contract, the signatory government could disregard it if the need arose. Unsurprisingly, such statements were poorly received, with the result that those on the other side insisted on the financing and other material contracts being governed by the laws of a jurisdiction that recognized the sanctity of contracts and the need for strict enforcement. The two governing laws most favoured to accomplish this were the laws of the world's two major financial centres: New York state, and England and Wales. This has not changed to this day, although I have sometimes been able to have natural resource projects outside of Canada partly governed by the laws of Ontario. Toronto and London are the world's two major mining financial centres, and Ontario's laws are not considered creditor adverse. Interestingly, over the years, I discovered that many Anglo-American lawyers have a gnawing doubt as to whether legal systems grounded in civil law, particularly continental European ones, would be as unwavering as the laws of the world's two major financial centres.

JAPANESE POSITIVENESS

The Japanese I dealt with strived to maintain a positive negotiating attitude at all times. They never missed an opportunity to remind everyone at the negotiating table of the main reason why the parties were negotiating. They also downplayed disagreements between the parties and emphasized those areas where there was agreement, all the while reminding everyone of the benefits of concluding the transaction. In other words, they regularly returned to the central purpose of the negotiations. I have tried to emulate my Japanese clients' patient attitude when negotiating, but must admit that I was not always able to do so with the same grace and consistency.

JAPANESE SILENCE

One of the first things I noticed in meetings was how the Japanese would often make a point or statement and then stop talking. The silence could last many seconds and even minutes depending on the context. This would often unnerve inexperienced Western negotiators. Westerners generally abhor silence in a conversational or negotiating setting and try to fill the gap. In fact, they often go further by talking over each other, something the Japanese, and many others, consider rude and disrespectful. In trying to fill the silence, Westerners more often than not undermined their position. The general rule in negotiations is that you make your point and then stop. It took a while to get accustomed to what I came to call the "Japanese silence."

Silence in the Japanese culture is a form of communication in itself and does not have the negative connotation that it may have in Western culture. Also, contrary to what some Western negotiators believe, silence was not a tactic to get Westerners to negotiate with themselves and otherwise make regretful statements. Depending on the context, silence has different meanings. Silence may be a sign of respect for the speaker by showing that his point was understood and is being carefully considered. In other instances, silence may be used to convey one's position in a non-verbal and possibly more sensitive manner. A short silence may signify acceptance of a position while a longer silence may underscore difficulty with that position. Silence may also be used to avoid conflict or say something that may embarrass the other side. Finally, silence allows the negotiators to read the room, think, and adjust their positions accordingly.

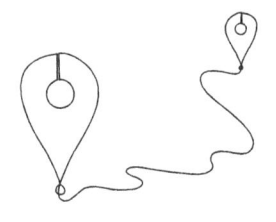

CHAPTER THREE

IDENTIFICATION, ALLOCATION, MITIGATION

KYOTO

My secondment with AMR ended late 1984. I left Tokyo and moved to Kyoto to try to improve my very limited Japanese, practise judo, and generally enjoy Japan at a slower pace. Shortly after my arrival, I came to live in a small family-owned traditional inn north of the Shichijō Bridge, close to the Kamo River, and not far from Kyoto's main train station. Within a radius of one hundred metres of the inn coexisted an interesting collection of neighbours: a small koban with its bicycle-riding policemen; the headquarters of the Kyoto branch of the Yamaguchi-gumi, Japan's largest yakuza family with its fleet of black Cadillacs coming and going; and a small children's park where, in times of tension among yakuza families, yakuza members would train in the dark of night, sometimes going as far as hanging punching bags from the swing set. Also within the inn's perimeter was a traditional bath house run by an old lady. In the late afternoon, the bathhouse would close and cater exclusively to the elaborately tattooed members of the yakuza. As a general rule, tattooed persons are excluded from public bathhouses and pools in Japan. By so restricting access to the bathhouse while the yakuza members were present, the old lady was preserving the respectability of her venerable neighbourhood institution.

CANADA

Toward the end of 1985, I decided it was time to come home, but I would slow-walk my return by spending six months in the Himalaya (Tibet, Nepal, and Ladakh) and Xinjiang. At the time, there was much Japanese interest in all things Silk Road, and Xinjiang was home to many of the more important stops along the road. Starting in 1980, and for the next ten years, NHK (Japan's state broadcaster) televised a series of documentaries on the Silk Road. The series was done in cooperation with China's national broadcaster and with the support of Chinese and Japanese political leaders, including Deng Xiaoping, the diminutive paramount leader of China from 1978 to 1989. The idea for the series was first broached by the Chinese in 1972 to improve China's image in Western countries — the same year US President Richard Nixon stunned the world by visiting China. That visit opened the path for other nations, including Japan, to do the same.

Japan's fascination with the Silk Road was not limited to television. In music, Kitarō became known around the world for his Silk Road Suite and Junya Sato's 1988 film *Silk Road* enjoyed critical acclaim as well as box office success.

I have wonderful memories from Xinjiang and the warm and open hospitality of its people, both Uighur and Han Chinese. I am extremely saddened by the tragic turn of events since then.

Once my sojourn concluded, I applied to a number of Canadian law firms. The Toronto office of SE offered me a place, provided I became qualified to practise in Ontario. I gratefully accepted and joined the firm as an articling student without any recognition for my prior experience. During my articles, I came to the realization that although Toronto was now the undisputed business capital of Canada, Montreal would be a better place for a francophone Canadian to develop an international practice. So I asked to transfer to the SE Montreal office once I qualified in Ontario. SE Montreal accepted, and I started in the fall of 1987, just in time to witness Black Monday, the stock market meltdown of October 19 when the Dow Jones Industrial Average lost more than 22 percent of its value.

On a more positive personal note, I was invited a year later, quite unexpectedly and without action on my part, to join the SE partnership. I would remain a partner until my retirement at the end of 2022.

RISK ANALYSIS

During my secondment to AMR, I developed basic legal skills. At SE I improved those skills and became more proficient at dealing with transaction risks. In so doing, I came to use a very simple analytical framework that could easily be remembered and explained:

In any transaction, each side must:

1. Identify the transaction risks

2. Allocate each transaction risk to the appropriate party

3. Manage each transaction risk by at least considering one or more of the following seven mitigants: law, due diligence, project structure, contract, security, credit enhancement, and insurance

The framework is apposite to all manner of transactions from the purchase of an appliance at your favourite big-box store to the engineering, construction, operation, and maintenance of an aluminum smelter, container port or railroad. In this book, I draw from my experience dealing with large, long-duration transactions because they are the ones that present the largest array of risks in a single transaction and consequently require the most forethought. This is especially true when limited recourse debt is used to finance the project and the financiers and other participants rely in whole, or in part, on the cashflows from the project. Said cashflows must be sufficient at all times after project commissioning to generate revenues sufficient to repay the project's debt, pay the project's expenses, and provide a reasonable return to the project's equity providers.

RISK IDENTIFICATION

It is best practice in major transactions for each party to hire legal, technical, and financial advisers to assist with the transaction. Other more specialized advisers may be hired, depending on the features of the transaction. When a party departs from such practice, it is recommended to visit with the client to understand the reasons for such departure. Failure to be properly assisted increases transaction risks.

In one privatization in East Africa in the 2010s, our client—a government—refused to hire technical and financial advisers despite our strong recommendation to do so. The client was of the opinion that, as owner and operator of the relevant business, it possessed all necessary technical expertise. We were also informed that a financial adviser was unnecessary because monetary matters had been agreed upon prior to our involvement in the file. Imagine our surprise when it was announced at closing that monies payable to our client would be substantially increased. We learned a few days after the closing that our client had, at the last minute, threatened to hire my suggested financial adviser, a major international investment bank, unless more money was forthcoming. The other side, not wanting to delay the transaction, agreed to increase the price. Our client's team was probably quite pleased with its sharp tactic. But the lack of a financial adviser begs the question as to whether the final monetary consideration was a fair price. The fact that the other side acquiesced so quickly could suggest otherwise. Also, discussions as to price without external scrutiny can raise serious ethical issues.

One of the first things a party and its advisers do when analyzing risk is determine the time horizon of their analysis. In long-duration transactions, parties must look far into the future and try to anticipate the risks that the project may encounter in ten, twenty, or more years. The risks may be internal or external to the project. While it is not possible to precisely identify all risks, it is possible to identify broad risk categories and build into the documentation mechanisms to deal with the consequences, should they occur. In shorter-term transactions, the risk analysis will, by definition, cover a more limited time horizon. In most M&A transactions and public equity financings, the parties are primarily concerned with the short term and their risk analysis will accordingly be more limited.

Risks are habitually divided into two broad categories depending on whether they are deemed commercial or not. Non-commercial risks include political, legal, and macroeconomic risks. Appendices I and II briefly describe broad risk categories most common to long-duration projects.

Risk analyses tend to have a bias, conscious or unconscious. This bias is usually in favour of the transaction. The first places bias shows up are in project assumptions, the probability of a risk occurring, and the ability to manage the risk. I used to repeat to myself, and anyone within earshot, that wishful thinking, magical realism, or other wondrous thinking were the fathers of project assumptions, and project assumptions were the mothers of screw-ups. Anyone reading the assumptions on which many government budgets are made would understand.

Time after time, I have seen projects run into difficulty because a risk had been poorly dealt with during project conception or structuring. There are numerous reasons for bias, including overconfidence, hubris, impatience, and project acquisition anxiety, but more often than not, it is the belief—often untethered to reality—that should a problem arise, it can be resolved at a later date. Some risks, commercial ones usually, can be resolved by further negotiation. It is generally costly, but it can be done; however, other risks, such as legal and regulatory risks, cannot be negotiated away after the fact. They pose difficulties that can lead to much loss and even project failure.

It is also very difficult to avoid bias if the advisers analyzing the project have a vested interest. Finding good advisers that are agnostic as to outcome is not always easy, particularly when the project's sponsors have a long pipeline of projects, and the advisers hope to garner future work. It is even more difficult when the advisers are being lobbied by a party to come to the "right" conclusion.

In one instance in the Persian Gulf, we had teamed up with highly regarded international financial and technical advisers to review a large infrastructure project on behalf of a government. The deal was very advanced, with much of the contractual, financial, and technical documentation nearly complete. In essence, we were being asked to provide a second opinion. On its face, the project looked sound, but once in-country, we quickly learned that it was the subject of considerable debate within the relevant ministry. Two factions, each with agendas and grievances that went far beyond the project's boundaries, were competing for our team's time and attention. One faction wanted to kill the project; the other wanted the project to go forward "as is," without any modification. In the parking lot, you could recognize those that belonged to one of the factions because they drove brand new cars. Our team was retained as a compromise and spent much of its time dealing with the arguments that were sometimes forcefully and stridently put forth by each side. Finally, within the allotted time, we submitted our report. After sufficient face-saving time had elapsed, and the arbitrary arrest and imprisonment of an engineer in a vain attempt to apply pressure on the "kill the project" side, the project was cancelled by the highest authority in the land. Needless to say, we did not make friends in that file. We never sought work again in that jurisdiction, knowing full well that it would be a lost cause. The whole episode also made me generally wary of second-opinion-type mandates.

RISK ALLOCATION

Once a risk has been identified, it needs to be allocated to the appropriate party. A risk is generally allocated to the party best able to manage it, in other words, the party best able to prevent its occurrence or, at the very least, best able to mitigate the consequences of such risk. If no party is able to manage the risk, it is then allocated to the party best able to withstand the consequences of such risk. This usually means the risk goes to the party with the deepest financial resources.

Exceptionally, a risk may be allocated to all the parties to the transaction with each party required to bear its own consequences of the risk. This is the case when the risk event is deemed irresistible and beyond the control of all the parties. In such cases, the assumption of the risk is twinned with contractual or legal relief. The types of relief granted are diverse and may range from total exoneration from the consequences of the event to the extension of delays to compensate for interruptions due to the event or increased payments to compensate for increased costs arising from the event.

In long-duration projects, particularly those that are financed on a limited recourse basis, it is essential to the viability of the project that the risk allocation be bankable—that is to say, acceptable to the financiers of the project. An allocation of a material risk to the wrong party will mean that the project is flawed and not financeable as it would threaten the continuity of the cashflow from the project.

In shorter duration projects, the relative strength of the parties to the transaction and exogenous factors will play a larger role in the allocation of risks; however, even here an odd risk allocation may indicate a problem and be cause to proceed with caution. For example, a seller willing to provide the buyer with "too good to be true" warranties and representations is usually an indication that the seller will not make good, or be unable to make good, on its obligations when the time comes.

RISK MITIGATION

For ease of analysis, I have divided risk mitigants into seven broad categories. The mitigation of a risk will involve a party and its advisers progressing through all seven categories and settling on a combination thereof.

Below I briefly describe each mitigant:

LAW: The laws applicable to a transaction are the foundations on which risk mitigation strategies are erected. It is essential that each party be conversant with such laws. The foregoing would seem self-evident; however, during my career, I have observed many risks dealt with a less-than-perfect knowledge of the laws applicable to such risks and their allocation and mitigation. Many lawyers over time become better versed in the contractual precedents from which they regularly negotiate than they are in the applicable laws. As a result, their first instinct is to revert to their precedent and try to cobble a contractual response rather than first determine whether the applicable laws provide a solution. Before a lawyer starts to write pregnant legal prose, ask the lawyer to briefly explain the applicable laws. Proceeding otherwise can delay negotiations and increase costs. The fact that lawyers are often under very tight time constraints does not help.

In one transaction on which I worked, the Ontario-based financiers of a Quebec PPP wanted payment assurances from the Quebec authorities. The Quebec authorities acquiesced and delivered assurances using their habitual format. The financiers rejected the Quebec format because they were unfamiliar with it, and it was governed by the laws of Quebec. They insisted on a version ordinarily delivered by Ontario authorities. When Quebec objected, the Ontario side firmly held its position. The amusing thing here was that the Quebec lawyers for all parties unanimously agreed that the model provided by Quebec delivered more security for the creditors. In the end, bewildered Quebec functionaries relented and used the Ontario model, but the needless tug of war materially delayed the closing of the transaction and produced a lesser result for the PPP's financiers.

It is not uncommon for some transactions to involve the laws of two or more jurisdictions. There are many reasons for this, including common ones, such as the parties being from different jurisdictions or the relevant assets being located in more than one jurisdiction. When a transaction is subject to more than one governing law, input from a multiplicity of lawyers is required. This adds a degree of complexity to the transaction, transaction costs are increased, and the timeline is lengthened. Notwithstanding these inconveniences, it is to each party's advantage to have a grasp of the applicable laws and how they interplay.

Aside from knowing the applicable laws, it is also necessary to know whether they will be enforced and, if so, how such enforcement will be carried out. In many jurisdictions, laws may be on the books but are poorly, if ever, enforced. This is common in lesser-developed countries due to a number of reasons, including corruption, inadequate resources, or lack of competent personnel. Each of the above reasons is a source of risk in itself, requiring analysis.

Lax and uneven enforcement may also be a factor in more economically developed countries. Canada, for example, is often criticized by the OECD and others for its very poor record at combatting financial crimes, including foreign corruption and money laundering. Financial crimes require considerable resources to detect, investigate, and prosecute, and the Canadian electorate is not clamouring for enforcement. In fact, there is much incentive for Canada to tread gingerly as Toronto is one of the world's principal bourses for extractive industries, with many foreign companies listed there. As for money laundering, Canada's economy is first and foremost a facile demographic play with immigration and inward investments being key to the health of the economy. As a result, Canadian authorities are relatively nonchalant when dealing with capital flows.

How laws are modified is also relevant. The stability and predictability of the legal environment surrounding a transaction is an important risk to consider as we shall see in Chapter Four.

In many instances, the law will be silent or uncertain on an issue material to a project. When the project is sufficiently important, most jurisdictions will adopt the necessary legal instrument to remedy the situation. In Canada and elsewhere, we have aided the process as required, often drafting and submitting for adoption the text of the law or regulation we thought was required for the project to be bankable.

DUE DILIGENCE: The phrase "due diligence" is used here in the broadest sense and includes any investigation, study, analysis, examination, and so forth, relating to a transaction. The importance and benefits of due diligence cannot be sufficiently stressed. In my experience, this is the most effective mitigant after law and, if well executed, offers great value for money. Unfortunately, deal makers often press forward notwithstanding incomplete or unsatisfactory due diligence. This propensity to proceed quickly is particularly prevalent in inflationary periods or when money is nearly free as in the period from 2010 to 2020 when interest rates on major currencies were historically low.

PROJECT STRUCTURE: The structure of a transaction has great bearing on risks. There is an old adage that the best way to mitigate a risk is by structuring it out of the transaction—in other words, by ensuring that the project structure does not generate the risk in the first place. I fully subscribe to that point of view. Also, in my experience, the more streamlined a structure, the more effective it is.

One of the concerns with overly complicated structures in long-duration transactions is that over the course of a project, the risk of an important element being ignored increases with time, often leading to failure of the structure. This is particularly true of complex payment and tax structures that after a few years end up being honoured in the breach because those using the structure forget its purpose and benefits and only notice the inconveniences.

CONTRACTS: Transactions need to be memorialized. Contracts and other project documentation set out the particulars of the project, the rights and obligations of the parties, and the remedies for breach of contract. Well written contracts provide an unambiguous record of the bargain reached among the parties and by doing so, minimize disputes and promote fairness. While contracts should set out the deal terms and conditions, my preference is that they be suppletive of the law; however, in some legal traditions, particularly the Anglo-American tradition, lawyers write such fulsome contracts as to appear to supplant rather than supplement the applicable law. Although documentation of this type has the not inconsequential benefit of removing a lot of uncertainty, it can be difficult to understand and negotiate. Their sheer size can be overwhelming as to make them indigestible and incomprehensible except to the initiated. This can slow down negotiations, particularly with governments and SOEs with lesser institutional capabilities. Voluminous documentation also introduces documentation risk. This is the risk that the various bits of paper do not dovetail with each other perfectly and are perhaps even contradictory.

SECURITY: Security is an essential tool. It incentivizes the party giving the security to perform its legal and contractual obligations. In large projects, it also allows the creditors to restructure a project by taking it over. There are numerous forms of security. Some stem from the law, such as mortgages, hypothecs, liens, privileges, pledges, and garnishments. Others are created by contract, such as performance bonds, purchase price holdbacks, escrows, offshore accounts, and voting trusts. In all cases, for security to be effective, it must be simple to use and provide fast relief. That is why, for example, bank letters of credit are often preferred over performance bonds because they are easier to use.

CREDIT ENHANCEMENT: In many transactions, the credit worthiness of a party is insufficient to ensure performance by such party. As a result, project risks cannot be realistically allocated to such party unless creditworthiness is enhanced, often by a third-party guarantee. This party could be a related entity, such as a parent company with substantial assets, or an entity that provides such service for a fee.

INSURANCE: Insurance is an effective mitigant for a broad range of risks. In addition to the casualty and liability risks of a project, insurance can mitigate material non-commercial risks, such as confiscation and expropriation, war and civil disturbance, breach of contract, failure to honour financial obligations, currency inconvertibility, and currency transfer restrictions. Also, the due diligence that insurers perform can be very informative as to the bankability of a project. When using insurance, it is important to be mindful of documentation risk—that is, the risk of mismatch between the contractual documentation among the parties and the terms and conditions of the insurance policies. Insurance is a very specialized field and should be handled accordingly through expert eyes.

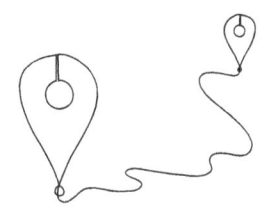

CHAPTER FOUR

STABILITY AND PREDICTABILITY

Foreign and domestic investors require stable and predictable investment environments. Stability and predictability does not mean immutability. Investors understand that changes may occur. However, such changes should be reasonable and evolutionary, not revolutionary. Moreover, investors must be able to discuss with the authorities the consequences, intended and unintended, of such changes. Finally, investors must have sufficient time to adapt their businesses to the new environment in a commercially reasonable manner.

The sad truth, however, is that government after government, whether from the left or right, in both rich and poor countries, keep breaching the stability and predictability rule. This hurts not only businesses and investors but society as a whole, particularly in lesser-developed countries where the impact of project delays and cancelations is felt more dearly, and the authorities do not have the means to soften the consequences of their mistakes.

In the 1980s and 1990s, it was common in less stable and predictable jurisdictions to enclave large foreign investments by creating special legal, tax, accounting, and other regimes for the investments. These special regimes would then be "stabilized" by treaty or contract with the relevant authorities, thus greatly reducing the risk that the authorities could legally modify or terminate the special regime without the consent of the relevant parties. This solution, however, created practical and ethical challenges for the host jurisdiction and is somewhat out of favour.

The multiplicity of regimes, often with different terms and conditions, resulted in a greater administrative burden and a lack of equal treatment among investors. This then encouraged investors to compare regimes and try to improve their own by pointing out the better terms and conditions given to other investors and applying pressure on the authorities. Special regimes also raised serious ethical issues as to how the regimes were negotiated, approved, and modified.

More recently, IFIs and better foreign investors recommend that jurisdictions adopt laws of general application designed to provide equal and fair treatment among investors, as well as more objective and transparent conditions regarding the permitting and licensing of projects and the investment protections afforded investors. This is the right approach for most jurisdictions, but in some more turbulent spots, it leaves projects exposed to the political vagaries of their host jurisdictions. In these cases, enclaving projects may continue to be an effective risk mitigation strategy.

The world grows ever more interconnected and the solutions to many challenges, including climate change, illegal immigration, and water availability are transnational and will require trillions of US dollars over time. These sums are far beyond the current capabilities of most countries and regions. Economic growth is necessary everywhere to help tackle these challenges and counter their root causes. The need for governments to foster sound economic growth through stable and predictable environments is no longer just a national or domestic matter, but one that transcends international borders. How do you discourage illegal migration if the migrants have no economic future or inhabitable environment in their country of origin?

Below are two examples highlighting the impact of instability and unpredictability and how fragile investor sentiment can be. In Guinea, the development of the world's largest untapped iron ore deposit, a project dear to the government since independence in 1958 and capable of doubling the GDP of Guinea, has been on hold for two generations. In Chile, recent unrest and constitutional uncertainty have caused domestic investors to doubt the future promise of one of South America's best performing economies.

GUINEA

In the fall of 1987, Naby Conte, a middle-aged Guinean jurist living in Canada, asked to visit with Courtois. In a surprising move, Courtois had joined SE from CCPT a few years before. Conte wanted to encourage SE to express interest in a World Bank initiative to improve Guinea's legal system. Guinea had been a turbulent French colony and an important first mover in the decolonization of Africa, but its first quarter century as an independent nation had left the country exhausted and, by most social indicators, little improved.

In 1958, General Charles de Gaulle, then president of France, proposed a new constitution for France, including the option for France's sub-Saharan colonies to become fully independent or have partial autonomy within a community of nations led by France. Each colony would hold a referendum to decide the way forward. France's preference was that the colonies would opt for partial autonomy. Guinea held its referendum on September 28, 1958. The result of the referendum was unfavourable to France. It was the only colony to opt for outright independence. On October 2, 1958, Guinea unilaterally declared independence. Guinea's bold move would eventually be the death knell of France's sub-Saharan empire. Within two years, most of France's colonies in the region had negotiated their independence.

Guinea's unilateral declaration of independence angered France. To demonstrate its displeasure and dissuade others from following in Guinea's footsteps, France quickly adopted several countermeasures. It abruptly pulled its civil servants, technical experts, and military presence out of the newly minted African nation and withdrew much equipment and other materiel, going as far as removing the bulbs from some streetlights. It also cut off all financial assistance and took steps to impede Guinea's external trade.

In turn, Guinea expelled French citizens and nationalized key industries, including mining, banking, and transportation. As a symbol of its desire for economic self-reliance, Guinea created its own currency, the Guinean franc, and in 1960 stopped using the CFA franc.

The CFA franc is the name of two currencies still used in most francophone sub-Saharan countries more than sixty years after independence: the West African CFA franc is used by eight countries and the Central African CFA franc by six countries. Both currencies have a fixed rate of exchange to the euro, and the central bank of each user country must deposit half of its foreign currency reserves with the French treasury.

The arrangement facilitates exchanges between France and its former colonies, but has been heavily criticized for encroaching upon the economic and monetary sovereignty of its users and effectively creating a commercial *chasse gardée* in a large swath of Africa. But the times are changing, and in 2020, France and its former West African colonies agreed to replace the West African CFA franc with the eco, a new currency to be used by the fifteen-nation Economic Community of West African States (ECOWAS). The political and economic instability of some ECOWAS members, however, has delayed the launch of the new currency to 2027, with further postponement quite likely.

Sékou Touré was Guinea's first president. He had been a key figure in Guinea's struggle for independence and would remain Guinea's president until his death in 1984. Touré was a charismatic politician who espoused a tough brand of "African socialism." Touré was but one of a long line of African leaders from that era who implemented variants of African socialism, including Julius Nyerere in Tanzania, Kenneth Kaunda in Zambia, and Kwame Nkrumah in Ghana. Touré had a strong authoritarian streak, and his governments were poor economic managers. As the years passed, and the consequences of Guinea's economic mismanagement grew, his single party regime increased repression and human rights abuses. Abroad, Touré was a proponent of non-alignment with a strong dose of anti-colonialism. Guinea's foreign policy during the Touré years was sympathetic to the USSR and estranged from the West. Guinea, in turn, received development aid and technical assistance primarily from the USSR and its allies.

Upon Touré's death, a military junta took over from which emerged Lansana Conté, a military officer, who would become the country's president for twenty-two years until his death in 2008, at which time another military junta led by Moïse Dadis Camara took over. Guinea would get its first freely elected president, Alpha Condé, in 2010, fifty-two years after independence. Condé, after promising to root out corruption and provide good government, held on to power through controversial and abusive means until he was deposed in 2021 in a military coup headed by Mamady Doumbouya, a special forces officer and former French legionnaire. Guinea's recent leadership history is by no means unique, and such sad stories exist on all continents.

In 1984, Guinea was in economic disrepair, and Touré's death allowed for a reset of the country's policies. Among other things, the new government sought to improve relations with the West, the World Bank, and other IFIs to repair the economy and attract foreign investment and know-how.

Guinea is blessed — or cursed — with large natural resources. In 1987, Canada's interest in Guinea centred around bauxite. Guinea was and continues to be one of the world's largest producers and exporters of bauxite, a key input in the production of aluminum. Alcan, then one of Canada's best-known multinationals — with its global headquarters in Montreal — was one of the shareholders, along with Guinea and others, in the Compagnie des Bauxites de Guinée (CBG). CBG operated the Boké mine, one of Guinea's two largest bauxite mines.

The mine is close to the port city of Kamsar. The city served as CBG's administrative headquarters, and a large number of Canadian and other expatriates lived there with their families. Kamsar is located about 140 kilometres from Conakry, the country's capital, and was in 1987 — thanks to CBG — a community endowed with services not commonly available to most Guineans or, for that matter, most Africans.

But Conté had approached Courtois because of iron, not bauxite. Guinea's iron ore deposits located in the Simandou mountain range in the southeastern corner of Guinea, not far from Sierra Leone and Liberia, remain the largest untapped iron ore deposits in the world. Since independence, Guinea has attempted to develop, alone or with others, its Simandou iron ore reserves. The project has been delayed for more than six decades in large part by unfavourable developments inside Guinea, including abrupt changes in government, arbitrary and erratic government decisions, and corruption. Guinea's lack of stability and predictability has caused the project to be modified often, with each modification creating a new set of challenges for prospective investors and opportunities for bad behaviour by officials.

At the time of Conté's visit, Courtois had been representing parties interested in the Simandou project for about a decade and had met with Touré on several occasions. Courtois agreed to meet with Conté and invited me to participate. At the end of the meeting, it was decided that I would research the matter further and speak with Canadian officials in Ottawa and at the World Bank. After much running around and fumbling, I concluded that the Canadian authorities were surprised, if not somewhat suspicious, that a Canadian law firm would be interested in institution building in Guinea. As for the World Bank, those in charge of the project tried, in a firm and somewhat patronizing manner, to dissuade us from exploring the matter further and declared that our chances of winning the mandate were negligible.

Undeterred, Courtois decided that we should go to Washington, DC, and visit the World Bank to see for ourselves. In Washington, we met with the World Bank Canadian executive director, who represents the interest of Canada and, at the time, those of Ireland and a number of Caribbean nations. The meeting was polite, but went nowhere. In fact, when we came out, we had the very distinct impression that the director was unconvinced about our motives or chances.

After the Canadian executive director meeting, we had a far more successful and encouraging meeting with the permanent staff of his office. The senior members of that office were Canadian and knew of the project. More importantly, they were happy to see a Canadian law firm showing interest. We were a welcome change from bossy engineering firms and consultancies demanding their "fair share" of World Bank projects and looking for scapegoats when they were unsuccessful. The fact that we were the only Canadians remotely interested also helped since it allowed the staff to be partisan and push harder.

Upon our return to Montreal, and after further consultations with the Canadian permanent staff at the World Bank, it was decided that I would head out to Conakry to gauge the opportunity further and present our credentials to the World Bank country resident, as well as various relevant Guinean ministries.

I flew to Brussels on Sabena, Belgium's now defunct airline, and then connected to that same airline's flight to

Dakar, Senegal, with a short stopover in Conakry. I got off in Conakry. The plane was full, but only a handful of us disembarked. I surmised from the facial expressions of the passengers that Conakry was not a popular destination. I came down the ramp and made my way on the tarmac to the airport terminal in the hot humid air of the airport. The terminal was a modern affair that had only recently been completed, but unfortunately, it was already showing signs of neglect. More ominously was the carcass of a Soviet-era passenger plane that was quietly decaying at the end of the runway.

Before I reached the terminal, a police officer accosted me and asked if he could be of assistance. Not being versed in the local ways, I frowned and asked what he meant. He said that the transportation situation being what it was, he could, after his shifts, place his police car and himself at my disposal.

Under the circumstances, his proposition seemed perfectly rational. After a little haggling, we agreed on a price and proceeded to walk out of the airport, bypassing all formalities except for the medical hut where all disembarking passengers had to proceed and show their vaccination booklet before entering the country. Most of the passengers, including myself, had not brought this document. In any event, the foreigners who had the booklet on their person were deemed missing the relevant vaccination. It was a scam and the "fine" for those without a booklet was US$20. If you did not want to pay the fine, you could be jabbed with some mystery liquid. HIV and AIDS were making headlines in the West with Africa, and Guinea in particular, being closely associated with the disease. The last thing one wanted was to be pricked with some needle on the side of a runway. I, along with everyone ahead of me in the line, paid the fine.

On my way into Conakry in the back of a police car, I could not help noticing that the city was a total mess. Numerous buildings were decrepit and many without roofs had luxuriating vegetation overflowing from them. They nonetheless were occupied, with smoke slowly rising from cooking fires.

The ride from the airport was a procession of one desolate scene after another, and it took some time to reach my destination: the Grand Hôtel de l'Indépendance (GHI). With its seven storeys, GHI was a very large structure for Conakry. It had been built in 1954 and opened as the Hôtel de France before changing its name at independence and adorning sometime thereafter a postage stamp as one of Guinea's symbols of modernity. When I was there, it had clearly seen better days.

In the early 1960s and 1970s, with the shackles of colonization removed, at least politically and administratively if not economically, the future seemed hopeful if not bright in much of sub-Saharan Africa. There was much to do in the newly independent countries, and the new governments seemed keen to get on with the job of nation building. Many of the newly independent countries had heterogeneous populations who, for decades — if not longer — had found common cause against their colonial powers, but otherwise had little in common.

Unfortunately, in many newly minted countries, the elites' first order of the day was to concentrate on dubious and self-serving nation-building symbols: presidential palaces, monuments, hotels, national sport stadiums, and so on. So they built symbols of modernity in their capitals that in most cases primarily served their needs and egos rather than the needs of the general population. We know from the numerous failures, and the few success stories of the last six decades, that while nation-building symbols are important, there are more effective ways to rally often diverse populations to a common purpose.

GHI, even in its relatively tired state, was an oasis for foreign travellers. In the quiet hotel restaurant, you could find an extraordinary brochette of individuals from all over the world, including North Koreans wearing ill-fitting grey suits with Kim Jong Il lapel buttons. Most of the guests were European and surprisingly willing to share their frank opinions and impressions of the country. Few were positive. During my stay, the "scandal of the week" was about an island off Conakry being used as an illicit dumping ground for European toxic refuse brought in by sea with the tacit complicity of government officials.

Communications were difficult in Conakry at the time. The phones barely worked, so I had to improvise. At night, I would handwrite letters on SE stationary, introducing the firm, stating my purpose, and requesting a meeting. When appropriate, I would attach relevant descriptive material. First thing in the morning, my friendly police officer would pick up the letters and proceed to the relevant offices. In the early afternoon, he would retrace the morning route and return with answers as to visits and time. Surprisingly, just about everyone agreed to meet, even on such short notice—probably out of politeness and curiosity rather than real interest. But, nonetheless, each visit was an opportunity to learn and cross-verify. The fact that the letters were being delivered by a police officer driving an official police car might have lent some gravitas to the exercise.

Among the things I learned from many of the NGO and aid expatriates was that Guinea had a nasty reputation in the bilateral and multilateral development assistance world. It was one of those countries, Haiti being another, that could rapidly stunt a career. So, in Guinea, you found more than a fair share of younger aid professionals or those at the end of their career patiently waiting for their pension.

In those days, Canada had an ambassador resident in Guinea. It made perfect sense. Alcan had major investments, and there were many Canadian expatriates at Kamsar, among other places. The embassy was a nice little compound amidst what I can only describe as a shanty town. The ambassador was a young francophone Canadian who had tired of Ottawa and literally asked to be sent anywhere. He told me: "Beware what you wish for." In any event, he was energetic and most helpful. He also had what is the number one attribute of any diplomat: a strong rolodex or contact list. He knew who to contact within the Guinean administration and civil society and could helpfully open doors.

After two weeks in Conakry, I returned to Canada much lighter. The many kilos of paper describing Canada, our firm, and its capabilities had been delivered. I wrote a summary of the trip and kept a watching brief on Guinea as part of our efforts in Africa.

Our interest in Guinea and its mining sector finally paid off in the mid-1990s when we won the first of several mandates related to mining. The mandates, funded by multilateral agencies, were fraught with difficulty as mining is the country's major foreign currency earner, and the country presents numerous political risks, including regional and domestic instability, weak institutions, overbearing foreign investors, and, last but certainly not least, corruption.

While I spent much time securing these mandates, I was also working on files in other countries and did not carry them out. The Guinea mandates were most ably carried out by others at SE, most notably by my former partners Jean Carrier and Viateur Chénard.

In 2022, Guinea, a Chinese consortium, and Rio Tinto—one of the world's largest mining corporations—announced that they would jointly develop mining blocks 1 and 2 of Simandou and that the project's configuration would include the construction and operation of the *TransGuinéen*, a more than 650 km railroad starting in the Simandou region and, after hugging the border with Liberia, ending at a port near Conakry.

This is a massive undertaking, well beyond the financial capabilities of Guinea. For Guinea, the *TransGuinéen* is a nation-building project that would serve several objectives, including opening up the interior of the country. This announcement is very promising as the project has the capacity to double the GDP of Guinea, one of the world's poorest countries. Whether the full potential of Simandou will ever be realized, and its benefits flow to the population, remains to be seen.

CHILE

I travelled to Chile in May 2022. Gabriel Boric, a former student leader, had just been sworn in as Chile's president on March 11, 2022, at the relatively young age of thirty-five. In 2022, Chile, an OECD member, had the third highest nominal GDP per capita in South America after Uruguay and Guyana. Other indicators were similarly favourable. Chile was nearly level with the US on Transparency International's Corruption Perception Index, and it remained an investment destination for foreign investors, including many US and Canadian companies. But Chile also has serious structural and societal issues, including growing wealth inequality, low wages and pensions, a rising cost of living, unequal access to higher education and health care, rising corruption, and land disputes with some Indigenous peoples.

In October 2019, an increase of thirty pesos (equivalent to about four US cents at the time) in the Santiago metro rush hour fares ignited a maelstrom of demonstrations and civil unrest. The demonstrations were led at first by students, but quickly spread to much of civil society, a bit like what happened in France with "Mai '68," which started in 1967 with university students complaining about female dormitory visit restrictions and grew to a near complete economic shutdown of France in May 1968.

The rapidly unfolding situation in Chile caught the political and business class totally unprepared. Unsympathetic statements by a minister suggesting that those who did not want to pay the increased fare only had to wake up earlier were out of touch and unhelpful. The unrest abated somewhat when the right-wing government of then President Piñera, a billionaire, reached an agreement with the opposition in November 2019 to reform Chile's 1980 constitution.

The 1980 constitution dates back to the Pinochet military regime and, although amended on many occasions by civilian governments, is an instrument that places considerable reliance on the individual, the family, private property, and the private sector. The 1980 constitution very much limits the role of the state. For example, the Chilean state cannot develop any entrepreneurial activity or participate in any such activity without being first expressly authorized by an absolute majority of both the Chamber of Deputies and the Senate of Chile.

The modification of the constitution by a Constitutional Convention was approved by plebiscite in October 2020 by a wide margin with the draft constitution to be submitted to a second plebiscite. In May 2021, the Chilean electorate was again solicited to elect the members of the 155-member Constitutional Convention. The elected members were primarily independents and representatives of left-leaning political parties.

The second plebiscite on the draft constitution was held on September 4, 2022. The draft was soundly rejected: Sixty-two percent of the votes cast were against the proposed constitution. The Boric government and the Constitutional Convention had seriously misread the mood of the electorate. The electorate had wanted change but, notwithstanding the intensity shown in public spaces, most wanted moderate change centred around bread-and-butter issues. The proposed constitution dealt with a plethora of issues that went far beyond the concerns of the majority of the electorate. The central issue for most of the electorate, especially the older generation, was how to reduce inequalities without hurting the economy.

In the aftermath of the 2022 plebiscite loss, a second constitutional process was agreed upon. A twenty-four-member commission of experts appointed by Congress would prepare the first draft of a proposed constitution. This draft would then be submitted to a Constitutional Council composed of twenty-five men and twenty-five women, who had been directly elected.

The government fully expected that the electorate would again elect a majority of members sympathetic to its objectives, but as is often the case in Chile, the electorate, in a balancing act, voted against the Boric government and elected a convention with a majority of members from the right. The second convention's proposal was submitted to a new plebiscite on December 17, 2023. That proposal was viewed as a step backward and soundly rejected — this time by nearly 56 percent of the votes cast.

Having failed twice, the government has decided to drop the matter for the time being. The two losses are by no means dispositive of the issue. It is fully expected that there will be constitutional change in the medium term, but how and when it will be carried out remains to be seen.

Notwithstanding the moderation shown by the Chilean electorate, the whole episode has chilled local investor sentiment. Chilean friends were quick to remind me that the rich and the not-so-rich in South America live by the 20/80 rule. Meaning that they keep 20 percent of their wealth in their country and 80 percent abroad in places like Panama City, Miami, Curaçao, and London.

For more than thirty years, Chile had been the exception that confirmed the rule, meaning that those who were economically successful had confidence in their country and viewed Chile as a stable and predictable investment destination. Chileans believed in the economic promise of their country and accordingly invested only a small fraction of their wealth abroad. The unrest of 2019–2021 and the arrival of Boric and his government, however, have ushered in an era where Chileans with means have begun to move capital outside Chile. This includes proceeds earned from the sales of businesses and assets to foreign investors still keen to invest in Chile and who, unlike local investors, are able to structure their investments to benefit from tax and investment protection treaties between Chile and their home jurisdiction.

In an age of growing polarization, the apparent search for a moderate solution by most of the Chilean electorate contrasts favourably with what has been going on in many other OECD countries. But then again, Chile has the advantage of living next to Argentina, a country that one hundred years ago was one of the wealthiest in the world but, thanks to ruinous and corrupt mismanagement, has become a highly indebted, runaway inflation jurisdiction about to embark on what may be an extraordinary economic experiment led by newly minted president, Javier Milei.

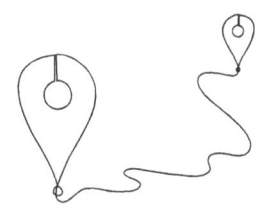

CHAPTER FIVE

COMMON OBJECTIVES

Many large, long-duration projects are joint ventures between two or more parties. Each party brings something to the venture: capital, know-how, markets, inputs, risk mitigation, and, in the case of IFIs and some major countries, the "halo effect" from having a very important investor or financier as part of the venture. The halo effect dissuades bad behaviour on the part of a project participant or host government. Few want to cross, and be blackballed by, an important world actor like the World Bank or the US, the European Union, China, or Japan. One never knows when the goodwill or assistance of such an important party will be required in the future.

A joint venture, by definition, requires all joint venturers to be on the same page as to the venture's objectives. All parties must row in the same direction or sing from the same music sheet. Failure to ensure from the outset that there is a clear agreement among the joint venturers as to the project's start-up phase, and thereafter, will eventually lead to protracted renegotiations or even termination of the venture as our five-year negotiations in each of Cuba and Chad amply demonstrate.

Both files involved joint ventures where the host country was one of the joint-venture parties and illustrated what happens when the parties use the same words but are not really on the same page. If a host jurisdiction's concerns are not adequately addressed by the signing of the final transaction documentation, the joint venture will be flawed and unstable, notwithstanding the smiles and handshakes at closing. The joint venture will then have to be rebalanced in the host jurisdiction's favour at the next opportune time. In the mining and oil and gas sector, this usually means the next time the commodity cycle is advantageous to producers.

In the Cuba file, the orthodox way of structuring and financing a large, long-duration project clashed with the aspirations and needs of a lesser economically developed economy. An established mining corporation wanted to apply traditional long-term finance solutions to its project while the host jurisdiction wanted maximum returns right away so as to meet the immediate needs of its population and government. One side preached patience, the other displayed impatience. Quite the dichotomy. How does one bridge the gap?

The first step is for the parties to recognize and acknowledge the disconnect between their respective positions. The second is to make sure the parties have the same understanding of words, concepts, and structures used in the negotiations. Definitions matter, and a didactic effort may be required.

The Cuban side was unfamiliar with Western accounting, taxation, mining regimes, and project financing structures. Lack of knowledge breeds mistrust, which in turn negatively impacts negotiations. As part of the negotiations, the mining corporation paid for third-party advisers selected by the Cuban government, but even this did not always speed things up. In the end, it became clear that the Cuban side wanted equal operating control and much "early" money. The foreign investor wanted to control the operations, immobilize as little equity as possible, and borrow as much project financing as the project could reasonably bear. The two positions being difficult to reconcile, the joint venture, despite final documentation having been signed, was never implemented.

The Chad file featured challenges similar to those in Cuba, as well as new ones. The World Bank was concerned about the ability of a small economy to absorb and deal efficiently with the very large revenues expected to come from oil production. It, therefore, tried to implement novel structures to ensure oil revenues would be used for the greater good. And though, unlike Cuba, the Chadian joint venture was built and is operating, despite assurances obtained after lengthy negotiations, the project has not developed in the manner that was first envisaged.

CUBA

Cuba was a long and fascinating personal experience. The brief consisted of advising an important Australian mining corporation in connection with the development and operation of what was projected to become the largest nickel and cobalt mine in Cuba and, by that fact, the most important foreign investment in Cuba. Nickel is one of

Cuba's major exports. The project was to develop a lateritic mine in eastern Cuba, but the negotiations were for the most part held in Havana. More than seven hundred kilometres separated the proposed mine site in Holguin province from the capital. Because of its size, the project was followed closely at the highest level in Cuba and abroad, including by Fidel Castro and the Miami-based anti-Castro leadership led by Jorge Mas Canosa. The senior members of the team met periodically with Castro, all the while receiving unsupportive letters from Canosa.

The file was acquired by SE in 1994 through a competitive process after William (Bill) Braithwaite, a future SE managing partner, suggested I put together a team and compete for this mandate from one of his clients. I had done some Quebec mining transaction work for the client and was a known quantity. The Montreal office put a presentation together, offered our services, and, after some delay, we were selected. The client's negotiating team was a collage of individuals and firms from around the world. There were Australian mining engineers and geologists, Mexican investment bankers, Dutch tax experts, UK insurance specialists, and Canadian and Chilean lawyers. Of course, there were no US citizens or US residents by reason of the US embargo — the Cubans deem it a blockade — and other US measures against Cuba.

Our client believed it was just a question of time before Cuba would follow former Eastern bloc countries down the path of economic liberalization. The fall of the Berlin Wall had unleashed a torrent of events that was quickly changing the world. Eastern bloc countries, such as Poland and Hungary, were embarking on large privatization programs and applying to join the European Union. Phrases like "the end of history" and "peace dividend" were being used with abandon by academics, bureaucrats, and politicians to reshape four-decade-old strategic thinking.

In the summer of 1961, the government of the German Democratic Republic, most often simply referred to as East Germany, decided to reinforce the border dividing East and West Berlin by erecting an "antifascist bulwark," better known as the Berlin Wall. That cement wall, replete with barbed wire, tumblers, and watch towers manned by guards with shoot to kill orders, stood for nearly thirty years as one of the most chilling and sad symbols of the Cold War.

On Thursday, November 9, 1989, the East German government announced that as of midnight that day East Germans could freely visit West Berlin. This was the culmination of months of social unrest in East Germany and elsewhere in the Warsaw Pact, the USSR-led counter to NATO. That weekend, two million East Germans visited West Berlin and feted their newfound freedom. During the festivities, something spontaneous and extraordinary happened. Germans on each side of the wall started to "peck" at the wall, eventually boring through it in places and even toppling it in parts. In a matter of hours, the wall went from being a symbol of repression to one of freedom. Berlin has since been sending bits of the wall around the world as gestures of goodwill. The fall of the Berlin Wall was the first of many events, including the reunification of Germany in October 1990, that would culminate in the dissolution of the USSR in December 1991, a geopolitical event whose repercussions continue to be felt around the world.

Cuba was a client state of the USSR. It received extensive financial, military, and other assistance from its patron. Cuba traded with the USSR on very favourable terms.

It was an effective proxy for the USSR in many African, Central American, and Caribbean nations. It sent legions of advisers abroad and fought in a number of wars on the African continent. The 1983 US invasion of Grenada was ostensibly to stop Cuban influence in that island nation and prevent any domino effect in the Caribbean Basin. Although Cuba was a member of the Soviet bloc, it benefited from a certain amount of wiggle room, a bit like Yugoslavia under Josip Tito. The ocean separating Moscow from Havana, Cuba's Taiwan-like position off the coast of the US, and Cuba's early membership in the Non-Aligned Movement were some of the reasons for Cuba's ability to act with some independence and of its own initiative. But it was first and foremost the international notoriety of Fidel Castro that gave Cuba the space for independent action.

Fidel Castro is one of three famous Cubans who were referred to only by their first name in Cuba and in much of the world. The other two are Che Guevara and Teo (Teofilo) Stevenson, Cuba's famous super-heavyweight boxer and gold medalist in the same weight division at three Olympic Games, starting with the 1972 Munich games. In Cuba, we were cautioned by Cubans and foreigners alike never to refer to Castro by name. Saying *El Jefe* while stroking one's chin or taping one's shoulder to indicate epaulettes sufficed.

Cuba effectively lost its patron in 1991 and entered a very difficult period euphemistically called the "Special Period." The economy was depressed, and restructuring was required. There was heavy rationing, and much was unavailable. The situation began to improve somewhat in the mid-1990s, but Cuba has never truly recovered and continues to suffer greatly from privations and self-inflicted wounds borne by poor economic stewardship and a lack of freedom.

Our client also hoped that in a few short years, the US would permit IFIs, most notably the World Bank and the Inter-American Development Bank, to assist Cuba in its development and even take an equity participation in the project or at least become a lender to it. This meant that the project would have to be structured in a way that would be easily recognizable to the IFIs and first-class international banks.

When negotiations for our client's project commenced in earnest in late 1994, Cuba was in its third year of the Special Period. The traffic during the day on the Malecon, Havana's famous corniche, consisted mostly of the odd "dromedary" (a truck with a box on its flatbed to house passengers), a few run-down taxis, and a small fleet of second-hand buses from around the world with their original colours and markings unchanged. Montreal was well represented in that fleet. Whenever I jogged in Havana, I would run on the more even road surface without fear of traffic.

Because we did not want to run afoul of US sanctions, we went to extraordinary lengths to ensure the property and services we used in Havana were clear of US claims. Our hotel was the Hotel Nacional de Cuba. The hotel was designed by the same architects as the Breakers in Palm Beach. The Nacional has a commanding view of Havana Bay and is a great place to have an after-dinner cigar. But the hotel was not selected for its amenities nor for its very colourful history; rather, it was selected because it was not on any US registry of expropriated properties. It was allegedly owned by US individuals before the revolution in

1959, but to our knowledge, no one ever filed a claim with the US authorities.

Another hotel with a similar pedigree is the Riviera, a Miami Art Deco–style hotel a stone's throw from the Nacional. It was opened in 1957 as a hotel and casino. Interestingly, Reuters reported in 2015 that descendants of Meyer Lansky, a man who served as inspiration for the character of Hyman Roth in Francis Coppola's *Godfather II* movie, were looking into the possibility of compensation from the Cuban government for the expropriation of the Riviera at the time of the revolution.

The same rigorous due diligence was carried out in relation to the mine site and any service provider or infrastructure to be used by the project. Any area or property whose title chain indicated previous US ownership was systematically excluded. Our client retained the services of a Cuban-American partner in a major Washington-based law firm to check US registries and carry out other due diligence. To make doubly sure that there would be no favourable bias, the client first confirmed that the US lawyer was well-considered in anti-Castro circles. All this fuss and attention to legal detail was a source of irritation for the Cuban authorities as they viewed the US embargo and other US restrictions as illegal and the expropriation or confiscation of property owned by US persons as lawful indemnification for the damage caused by the US. For the Cuban side, our insistence on ownership due diligence was time wasting. The Cuban government has always insisted that the US blockade has cost Cuba dearly, and whenever the matter of reparations has been brought up by the US, Cuba has responded by exhibiting its own list of damages resulting from US action. As you can expect, the Cuban damage claim is greater than the US one.

Due diligence in Cuba was difficult. Aside from the secretive tendencies of the authorities and their different approach to private property and individual rights, there was the paucity of records. In many districts, pre-revolution land and other registries were poorly preserved, incomplete, and difficult to consult. This having been said, I can understand why little attention was spared for what had become, in the eyes of most Cubans, meaningless records of a bygone era.

We were negotiating with the Ministry of Basic Industries (Minbas). Minbas had a very broad portfolio and was in charge of electricity, oil, nickel, cement, and pharmaceuticals, among other things. Minbas was under the leadership of Marcos Portal, one of Cuba's most influential ministers. Portal was both truly capable and connected. He was married to one of Castro's nieces and, more relevantly, was a member of the Council of State as well as the politburo.

On one occasion, I was able to sample his powerful reach. It was summer, and I had arrived at Havana's José Martí International Airport by myself from Nassau, Bahamas, on a chartered twin engine propeller plane. At immigration, I could not find my passport, and after a few minutes of searching my luggage, I gave up and simply informed the immigration officer that I was working with Minbas and Portal's office. He asked for the number of Portal's office and went away. After ten minutes, the officer came back with a laissez-passer and, relieved, I quickly exited the terminal and proceeded to join the taxi line.

The Cuban negotiating team was bright and committed. Most were graduates of the University of Havana, but some had been educated in the USSR. This generally meant considerable personal sacrifice as they would first have to spend a few years learning Russian in Moscow before enrolling in their program in Moscow or Leningrad or further afield if less fortunate.

Surprisingly, a few ancillary members of the Cuban team were dual US and Cuban citizens who could freely go to the US and did so to visit their families—and came back with full suitcases—but otherwise stayed in Havana for personal reasons. When asked why they did not move to the US, they usually answered that they preferred the warmth and solidarity of Cuban society. I got the sense that their answers were genuine. One of the more sympathetic members of the Cuban team was an interpreter who worked for the Cuban side from time to time. He had been Cuba's official Mongolian-to-Spanish interpreter. After the fall of the USSR, he had come to the realization that there might be a brighter future if he became proficient in English, Mongolian being of limited use in the Caribbean Basin.

The situation in Havana in the mid-1990s was still controlled. The government had not yet opened much of the economy to small businesses, and there was little noticeable petty corruption or street crime. Our contacts with the negotiating team were limited and somewhat choreographed and stilted, except of course at the senior level.

How the Cuban team interacted with us was heavily dependent on how the negotiations were going. The teams met monthly in Havana for at least one week and often for two. While the trip was relatively easy for those living in the Americas and Europe, it was a long and fatiguing journey for those coming in from Australia. When Cuba wanted to emphasize their displeasure with us, they would simply refuse to meet during our stay, appearing only an hour or so before our departure to the airport to apologize and present us with some pretext for their behaviour.

I have estimated that I have lived on the sixth floor of the Nacional for a year, probably more. The sixth floor was, for want of a better description, the Nacional's executive floor. Our office and conference rooms were on that floor, and there were many days when we would leave that floor only to meet for dinner on the ground floor.

Most negotiations were held on the sixth floor. The pace in Havana consisted of ten-hour days, and sometimes more for the lawyers as they would have to draft after all the meetings. On two-week trips, we would have a Sunday break. In more than fifty trips to Cuba, I went to the beach only one day.

Because of the need for confidentiality, our team included secretarial staff, who were equipped with first-generation portable computers. They were usually employees of SE. There was no shortage of volunteers. While it was literally no day at the beach, working in Cuba did offer a break from the Montreal routine and a little extra sunshine in the winter.

Two years into the project, I had a new volunteer. She was a middle-aged personal assistant from the Montreal office. Her story was out of the ordinary. When she was sixteen and living in the Quebec countryside, she met a Mexican and eloped with him to Mexico. She had a family with him there. They eventually split up, and she returned to Canada with the children. It had been twenty or so years since she had been to Mexico, and she was very keen to join the team if she could swing by Mexico City on her way to Cuba. That way, she would have an opportunity to reconnect with her Mexican family. I immediately acquiesced. How can you resist such a story?

Her first visit to Mexico was a great success, and she continued to pass through regularly for several years until the end of the project. She was very popular with the staff at the Nacional, and they freely gossiped with her, giving us a window into Cuban life and more. The Cubans nicknamed her "la Mexicana" on account of her strong Mexican accent.

Most of the project's commercial risks, such as demand, technology, engineering, construction, and so on, were manageable, even though it took constant work to remind the Cubans that the project would be engineered outside Cuba and that the critical equipment would likewise be manufactured abroad. The Cubans, with some justification, were quite confident in their engineering and scientific capabilities, but financiers were unlikely to be of the same opinion; however, there were two commercial risks that proved difficult to manage: the environment and staffing.

The Cubans viewed environmental protection as an expensive luxury. The Cuban side did not want to pollute, but in their view, it was the cost of earning valuable hard currency with which to buy food, medicine, and other life necessities. This led to the unusual spectacle of a private concern trying to impose high standards on itself and the government side doing the opposite. The real reason for the private sector's zeal was, of course, the bankability of the project. The project needed to adhere to modern environmental standards to be eligible for project financing, whether from IFIs or private lenders. A "dirty" project was simply not bankable. This whole episode brought home, in clear terms, the irony that much wealth and economic growth will be necessary to move away from our carbon-based economies.

The second risk was staffing. It was agreed that most of the workers would be Cuban and that the number of expatriates during operations would be small. But the Cubans insisted on the project adhering to their labour system for foreign investors. In that system, the investor contracted with a Cuban governmental agency to provide them with the necessary Cuban staff for which the investor would be charged a fee in hard currency. The governmental agency would then turn around and pay the Cuban staff in local currency a small portion of the hard currency fee paid by the foreign investor and keep the rest. This way of proceeding was wrong on so many levels, and our client did not want anything to do with it. It wanted a more traditional employer-employee relationship. It wanted to select its employees, pay them directly, and manage its work force without any intermediary. It took years to resolve this very important issue.

In the later years of the Cuba mining file, our involvement with Cuba became widely known among those interested in investing in the country. A number of foreign companies retained our services to better understand the practical side of transacting with Cuba.

In one case, a multinational household cleaning product manufacturer wanted to enter the market. In order to market its products, the manufacturer was planning on hiring about fifty sales ladies that would each drive a company car around their assigned district. This was the client's standard practice around the world. The Cubans agreed, but insisted that each car be assigned a driver, thus doubling the number of jobs. They also wanted significant control over the sales ladies, including tight control on samples to prevent their resale. It took a long time and much effort to sort this out. There were, of course, a handful of small Cuban business law firms, but these were effectively government entities where confidentiality and innovation were not necessarily priorities.

The list of Cuban political, legal, and macroeconomic risks was very long and included just about every category except, of course, anything to do with the normal exercise of political rights in a democracy, such as free speech and the right to strike. The Cuban legal, taxation, and accounting systems were ill-suited to accommodate a project of this size and, as a result, the project would have to have its own special regimes that involved investment, tax, accounting, and so on. It took two years to get this accepted and another two years to negotiate.

The most difficult regime to negotiate was the mining regime. Cuba, halfway through our negotiations, had adopted a new mining law. Unfortunately, the law, which we had never seen in draft form, created more problems than it solved. There were many awkward plenary sessions during which I had to painstakingly go through the law and demonstrate its inadequacy for the venture's purpose. I wanted to express our concerns in small committee but the Cuban side, always worried about the loyalty of its representatives, insisted on having everyone around the table. Needless to say, I was not popular with the authors of the law.

The last item that was negotiated was the international dispute resolution mechanism. It was in fact finally agreed upon only minutes before our leaving the Nacional for the signature ceremony at the Palace of the Revolution. The signing with Castro present made the nightly news in Cuba and was featured prominently in Cuban media. Sometime thereafter, Portal was awarded the highest civilian award he could receive as a minister.

In addition to non-commercial Cuban risks, the project had to contend with the extra-territorial application of US laws. No country extends the application of its laws beyond its borders as much as the US. On February 24, 1996, two MIGs from the Cuban Air Force intercepted three small Cessna planes off the coast of Cuba. Two planes were shot down without warning, and their four occupants were killed. The third plane returned to Florida.

The planes were operated by Brothers to the Rescue, a US-based anti-Cuban government organization. In the previous month, Brothers to the Rescue had flown close to Cuba and released pamphlets that had reached Havana. Furious, Cuba had warned the organization not to repeat their actions. Upon learning of the downing of the aircrafts, the Cuban-American community swiftly mobilized and demanded that the US take action against Cuba. President Clinton, who had been pursuing a policy of détente with Cuba, declared a national emergency on March 1, 1996. On March 6, 1996, Congress passed the Cuban Liberty and Democratic Solidarity Act (Libertad) of 1996 (Helms–Burton Act). Clinton signed it into law, with effect from March 12, 1996. The speed with which events unfolded is impressive, but it must be remembered that 1996 was a US presidential election year and, as is often the case with Democrat presidents, Clinton could not afford to appear weak. He had to take strong action.

The Helms–Burton Act is a wide-ranging law first proposed in 1995 by Republican Senator Jesse Helms. It had been filibustered by the Democrats and was going nowhere in Congress until the sad and unwarranted Cuban over-reaction of February 24, 1996. The Helms–Burton Act is purposefully written using broad and sometimes vague language and is difficult to interpret. It exposes foreign nationals and companies to private lawsuits in the US if they have "trafficked" in illegally expropriated property. Trafficking is broadly defined in the act and includes simple usage. The real purpose of the act was to make it cumbersome for anyone to do business in both the US and Cuba. This feature of the Helms-Burton Act did underscore the soundness of our client's due diligence efforts as to US ownership of Cuban property and their systematic exclusion from the project.

After the signing of the nickel project in 1998, I continued to work on the file from time to time until 2000. That year, it became crystal clear that Cuba, with its newfound benefactor — Venezuela's Hugo Chávez — would return to its old ways. The joint venture was then abandoned.

It had taken close to six years to realize that Cuba was willing to change only because of the loss of its patron, the USSR. Now that it had found a new benefactor, Cuba would return to its idiosyncratic path, supported by cheap Venezuelan oil in exchange for Cuban talent in the form of doctors, teachers, sport coaches, and security personnel — the latter now having become essential to the survival of the Venezuelan regime of President Nicolás Maduro.

CHAD

Chad was a file obtained via James Arnett in 1996. Arnett, who later became CEO of Molson Brewery (one of the two companies that merged to form Molson Coors Beverage Company), had been a co-managing partner of SE's Toronto office and was now the managing partner of SE's Washington office. He had learned that the World Bank would finance legal advisers to assist Chad in implementing a project where oil majors would develop oil fields near Doba, a city in the south of the country.

Because Chad is landlocked, the project would export the oil using a purpose-built pipeline that would run from Chad through Cameroon to finish at a floating storage vessel off the coast of the town of Kribi. As a result, the project required very large investments. Arnett first approached SE's Calgary office, followed by its Toronto office. Both declined. He then came to me in Montreal with about ten days left before submission date.

We quickly said yes and proceeded to prepare a proposal for consideration by Chad and its financier, the World Bank. The project was at the time sponsored by Exxon, Shell, and Elf. The last two would eventually be replaced by Petronas and Chevron. The ownership would later evolve further and include participations by Chad and Cameroon. The project, if properly structured, could greatly improve the life of Chadians. Chad was, and very much remains, one of the world's most impoverished countries. At the time, it was just coming out of more than twenty-five years of civil war. Its social indicators were abysmal. Most educated Chadians had long fled the country in search of peace and opportunity.

The project was outsized for Chad, and the World Bank was concerned that Chad's economy would have difficulty coping with a project of this size. The project was expected to generate yearly revenues of US$200 million for Chad. At the time, the GDP of Chad was approximately US$1.6 billion for a population a little over seven million.

The World Bank's projections turned out to be very conservative: The project has generated each year multiples of the first estimates. An influx of so much money raised concerns on two levels. The first was the macroeconomic ability of a small economy to absorb so much money without adverse consequences, inflation being one of them. The second was how to prevent such large amounts from being squandered. With Chad, the World Bank welcomed the opportunity to defeat the "paradox of oil"—a phrase meant to underscore the fact that despite significant oil revenues, most oil producers end up being poorer, less democratic, and more corrupt than countries without oil. Of course, there are exceptions, but they are few and far between.

To achieve its aim, the World Bank developed a model for sound oil revenue usage in Chad. As a condition to lending to the project and, by doing so, reassuring Exxon and the other foreign investors, the World Bank demanded that Chad adopt legislation essentially dividing oil revenues into four streams. First, a percentage would go to a fund for future generations. Second, the bulk of revenues would go to pay for health, education, infrastructure, and other development projects. Third, a percentage would go to benefit the oil-producing region. Fourth, the remaining 15 percent would go to the government's general fund. The whole would be supervised by an oversight committee to include members from civil society. Chad agreed to the above, and everyone working on the project was excited about the possibility of demonstrably showing a new path for resource rich nations.

The country's negotiating team had few individuals who had direct experience in the oil industry and pipelines. The industry was new to Chad, and the government was competing for talent with the better funded foreign investors. The matter of the negotiating team was further complicated by HIV and AIDS. The disease was ravaging the better-educated strata of society. Treatment of the disease was still in its infancy. In many countries, there was, and to some extent remains, a reluctance to declare oneself ill for fear of being shunned. As a result, there was a tendency among those who were ill to keep silent and keep working until unable to do so. They would then stay at home and leave their families to announce their death after a short absence.

AIDS was a considerable problem for the Chadian authorities. The disease decimated the country's negotiating team and affected the continuity of negotiations, particularly in 1996 and 1997.

Upon arriving in N'Djamena with Alain Massicotte, another SE partner, we learned that because of a death in his family, the project head of the Chadian side would not be able to see us for another week. With little else to do, we took the opportunity to acquaint ourselves better with our new client. In those days, connectivity from many countries, including Chad, was poor. If you were in-country before the project had started, the time was essentially yours. We were staying at the Novotel (the better hotel at the time) on the shore of the Chari River right in front of the main French military base as well as that of a number of camel-mounted Chadian soldiers. I had seen camel-mounted security forces before in the Persian Gulf and Rajasthan, India, but the Chadian's were particularly striking in their indigo turbans and clothes. They were very much like those depicted in Tintin adventures, minus the French colonial officer.

Personal security in N'Djamena in 1996 was uneven, to put it charitably. Massicotte and I were attacked once in broad daylight on the largest artery of the city and saved when a Chadian family in a Peugeot 404 opened the back door to their car, allowing us to dive in. The family very kindly returned us to our hotel. At night, if we wanted to go out, our driver would wait for a French military truck to exit from the neighbouring base, and we would follow it to whatever restaurant the French soldiers were visiting that evening. At the restaurant, you ate with purpose to be ready to closely follow the soldiers on the return leg. It made for smoother roadblock crossings. I celebrated my fortieth birthday in this manner.

Martin Scheim and Massicotte were the two SE partners who ably and patiently carried the file to final documentation in 2000, at which time our work was complete. Construction of the project began immediately thereafter, and the project was commissioned in 2003. The project has had its share of controversies. Among other things, the World Bank contends that the income allocation structure was not applied as designed and, as a result, has proven fragile.

According to observers, the idea behind the structure is fundamentally sound, but many lessons must be gleaned from the Chad experience to make such structures more robust, particularly when a country's elite chafes at not having full access to the revenues from the project. The fact that the project was so financially successful gave the country's leadership the opportunity to undo much of the work of the World Bank. When the World Bank complained, Chad simply prepaid many of its project loans to be free of World Bank supervision. Only the International Finance Corporation (IFC) refused repayment so it could continue to have a say.

Chad's strengthened negotiating position is not only grounded in money, but also in the geopolitics of a very unstable region. Chad has considerable cover and leeway as a result of its location at the centre of a difficult part of the world where the West has lost much ground, and Russia and non-state actors are making a play for power. Chad is viewed by France and the US as a friendly regime with an agile battle-hardened army effective at dealing with regional threats.

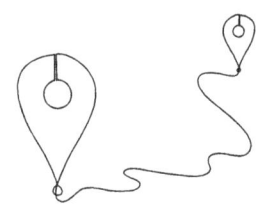

CHAPTER SIX

OPPORTUNITY

Opportunity often appears without notice from the least likely of situations. I have encountered many impecunious individuals with great ideas. We were able to accompany a few to successful outcomes, mostly in clean energy and infrastructure. But the opportunity with the greatest professional and fiscal impact came as a result of unrelated situations at opposite ends of the world: the export of electricity from Laos to Thailand and Hydro-Québec's strengthening of its electricity transmission network after the great ice storm of January 1998. The conditions for success smoothly coalesced: The timing was right, the assets had the appropriate features, the applicable law was helpful, the lawyers and investment bankers were willing to innovate, and, most important of all, the client was willing to experiment and see it through.

LAOS

It all started in Laos. My first working visit to that country was in 1993. The International Development Law Institute (now the International Law Development Organization), an international organization based in Rome whose motto is "Creating a Culture of Justice," was organizing a two-week seminar on negotiating with the private sector in Vientiane, the country's sleepy capital. Very few Westerners visited Vientiane in those days, just a few aid workers, diplomats, and backpackers.

Laos was not yet a tourist destination. The bridge across the Mekong, linking Vientiane to Thailand, was still a few years away, the road from Vientiane to Luang Prabang, a UNESCO world heritage site, was regularly cut off by Hmong insurgents, and the semi-high-speed rail linking Vientiane to China would not be completed for another three decades.

The language of the seminar was to be French, and IDLI thought it would be good to have a Quebec lawyer in addition to jurists from France and Belgium. IDLI approached Marc Lalonde and asked whether he could suggest someone. Prior to joining SE, Lalonde had a long and brilliant career in Canadian federal politics. Among other things, he had been Canada's first francophone federal Minister of Finance and one of the architects of Canada's health system. He approached me, and I immediately said yes, even though my desk was quite full.

Attendees were to be senior civil servants from Vietnam, Thailand, Laos, and Cambodia. In those days, there were numerous reasons why civil servants attended seminars. The daily stipends for out-of-pocket expenses were very much one of them. Attendees saved the stipends and bought goods at the end of the trip to bring back home. The stipends were a function of the cost of living at the seminar location. Vientiane had a low cost of living, and the stipends reflected that fact. Moreover, there was little to buy in the Lao People's Democratic Republic. IDLI had planned well. Attendance was strong, about forty senior civil servants, and the seminar was more of a working affair and less of a junket.

If the location of the seminar was fine, the language had become an issue. The Vietnamese delegation was comprised mostly of older individuals who had studied in French schools before independence in the North and reunification in the South. Some of the older Lao mastered French. But with the Thai and the Cambodians, French was little understood except for a few Cambodian returnees who had fled and taken refuge in France during Cambodia's genocidal Pol Pot regime. Nearly all the participants had some command of English, and it was decided that the course would be bilingual.

From 1967 to 1989, Cambodia, a small agrarian country, was unwittingly drawn into the Southeast Asian version of the Great Game. During that period, Cambodia experienced instability, unrest, genocide, and war on a countrywide scale. This state of affairs officially ended with the 1991 Comprehensive Cambodian Peace Agreements and the 1993 Cambodian elections organized by the United Nations Transitional Authority in Cambodia (UNTAC).

The Khmer Rouge, led by Pol Pot, were in power in Cambodia from 1975 to 1979 and perpetrated one of recorded history's worst genocides by a government on its people. While most of the world stood by quietly, and others like China provided the Pol Pot regime with diplomatic cover, the Khmer Rouge directly and indirectly killed one out of every four Cambodians. One of the most chilling places one can visit is Security Prison 21, home of the Tuol Sleng Genocide Museum in Phnom Penh. The movie *Killing Fields*, the 1984 adaption of the book *The Death and Life of Dith Pran*, is as good a place for a Westerner to start learning about this atrocity. The movie was nominated in seven categories at the 1984 Academy Awards and won three awards, including one for best supporting actor.

Only the 1979 invasion by Vietnam managed to put an end to the Khmer Rouge horrors, but Vietnam's occupation of Cambodia resulted in ten more years of fighting in both Cambodia and beyond its borders. Vietnam and China also fought a brief border war in 1979. The battle-hardened Vietnamese badly mauled an uncoordinated Chinese invading army. The defeat hammered home a hard lesson about military professionalism and the need for combined arms warfare that the Chinese have very much taken to heart ever since.

Because of the genocide and the subsequent war, many Cambodian participants were either much older or younger than the other delegations. Moreover, some clearly suffered from some form of PTSD. There were a lot of moments when members of the Cambodian delegation were doing the thousand-yard stare and would lose themselves in thought. You had to wait for them to return from their mental sojourn and rejoin the group.

I prepared a course that used examples of large and smaller projects gone wrong, with a balanced mixture of examples from developed and developing economies. I did not want to give the impression that problems arose only in the developing world.

My second work experience in Laos came in 1997, when SE won a mandate funded by the ADB to advise the Lao government in connection with the establishment of a high-voltage electricity transmission company. SE was the lead service provider, and we teamed up with Hydro-Québec International, the international arm of Hydro-Québec (HQ), and another sub-contractor. HQ is the state-owned electricity company of Quebec. It is one of the world's largest hydroelectricity producers, and its generation is nearly 100 percent renewable with only a few diesel generator sets in remote communities unconnected to its grid.

HQ operates a large transmission network and was at the forefront of some of the world's most important electricity transmission innovations, including the 730 kV high-voltage transmission lines invented in the early 1960s by Jean-Jacques Archambault, a young Quebec engineer.

In the 1990s, the Electricity Generating Authority of Thailand (EGAT), Thailand's HQ equivalent, was entering into power purchase agreements with independent power producers (IPP) that were developing hydroelectricity projects in Laos. The ADB and the Lao government were concerned that the projects were being developed in an uncoordinated fashion and, among other things, would result in a multitude of power lines wastefully crisscrossing each other without forethought. Moreover, the lines would have to cross the Mekong, Southeast Asia's great river, to reach EGAT's grid. If improperly built and maintained, the lines over the Mekong could have a material adverse impact on the river, including on navigation.

Our brief was to determine the conditions necessary to establish a national power grid company that could rationally transport the IPP production to Thailand as well as serve to provide power to much of Laos. We were equipped with a large office space in the Electricite du Laos building and a number of Lao professionals were seconded to the team, including a lawyer who, during Soviet times, had been sent for the better part of decade for Russian language training and legal education in Dushanbe, the capital of Tajikistan. The IPP promoters were generally skeptical of Laos's ability to set up and operate such a company by itself. To counter the skepticism and elicit comment that might prove useful, our first suggestion was to prominently install outside our office a large metal plaque clearly marked: "Lao National Grid Company."

Midway through our mandate, we were approached by a Lao government minister. He was an engineering graduate of the Université de Sherbrooke, Quebec. He asked whether it would be possible, as a courtesy, to hold study sessions for senior Lao civil servants on some troubling matters arising from the rapid development of IPPs in Laos. I acquiesced and was given English or French translations of a number of Lao laws to study. The following stratagem was of particular concern to the minister: A group of well-connected individuals would form a company with a view to applying for the right to develop a hydroelectric facility in a valley, preferably one with precious first growth tropical forests. Once the right had been granted, and any local population displaced, the company would log the valley and sell the wood to foreign buyers. The electricity project would then be abandoned. In other words, unscrupulous individuals were using the hydroelectricity development framework as cover to get around forestry laws, displace populations, hurt the environment, and make a lot of money. The study sessions, held early in the evening, were well attended and helped identify the framework's loopholes and ways to plug them. It would be very naive, however, to believe that the sessions would be effective in stopping the scams. Something much stronger would be required, and it came in the form of the 1997 Asian financial crisis.

The ADB Lao mandate lasted more than a year and required the team's presence in Laos every six or so weeks. At the time, there were few flights into Vientiane, and we had to overnight in Bangkok on our way in and out. On July 2, 1997, I happened to be in Bangkok on my way to Vientiane when the Central Bank of Thailand decided it would no longer defend the Thai currency. The Thai Baht would float freely. In a matter of hours, the Baht sank deeply against the US dollar, capital flight began, and the local stock market tanked. Within days, the financial crisis was infecting other Asian countries, most notably Indonesia and South Korea.

On the return leg through Bangkok seven days later, I noticed pamphlets being freely distributed just outside the gate of my hotel announcing fire sales by individuals. Luxury cars, watches, electronics, and so on were being sold for hard currency at pennies on the dollar. It reminded me of the famous 1929 market crash photo of the attractive two-door car with a sign on it: "$100 will buy this car. Must have cash. Lost all on the stock market." The 1997 Asian financial crisis at its apex was brutal. It hit three countries particularly hard: Thailand, South Korea, and Indonesia. In Indonesia, the crisis ended the thirty-two-year Suharto regime. Overnight, the 1997 Asian financial crisis changed the region's economic landscape, including the urgency that our report was addressing. The Lao IPP development temporarily slowed down to a crawl, giving the Lao government and its state-owned electricity company more time to deal with the issue of the national power grid company and some of the unintended consequences of IPP development, including unscrupulous deforestation.

THE GREAT ICE STORM OF 1998

In January 1998, a succession of five ice storms hit eastern Ontario, Quebec, New Brunswick, Nova Scotia, and US states bordering these provinces in what has since been named the Great Ice Storm of 1998. Around 130 mm of freezing rain fell over a period of five days, covering everything in its path with ice. Freezing rain is common in most of these areas, and infrastructure is engineered to deal with a normal storm. But the phenomenon of 1998 was extraordinary and adversely affected cities and infrastructure, most notably Quebec's power grid, leaving millions in the dark. The weight of the ice on power lines caused many transmission towers to crumble. Quebec is one of the few jurisdictions in the world where electricity is the preferred energy for home heating. Moreover, few dwellings have back-up heating sources should power be interrupted. The power failures left millions without heating in one of the coldest months of the year in one of the coldest countries in the world. Montreal in January is colder than Moscow, and Montreal is one of Quebec's southernmost cities! In support of provincial recovery efforts across eastern Canada, the federal government deployed more than 20 percent of the Canadian Armed Forces. The crisis lasted in most places for a week to ten days, but some areas were without power for up to three weeks.

In the aftermath of the crisis, the Quebec government ordered HQ to strengthen Quebec's electricity transmission network. It is in that context that HQ approached one of Quebec's few private power producers and asked to use its transmission network's rights of way to build new lines. The producer agreed. Although not a client of SE, the private producer invited us to make a presentation as part of a competitive process to provide legal representation in connection with the HQ right of way transaction.

In preparation for our presentation, we were provided with maps of the private electric system. One feature that quickly stood out was a power connection that crossed the Ottawa River, linking the private system with Ontario's power grid. The map reminded me of work being carried out in Laos and the proposed power lines crossing the Mekong toward EGAT's power grid. Because of the various legal and de facto monopolies enjoyed by HQ, it was highly unlikely that in modern times a private sector entity could replicate such a connection. The connection could provide operation and commercial flexibility, and we decided to take a closer look at the generating assets of the private system. We discovered that, because of their age, these assets had unique features that gave the private power producer considerable operational and regulatory autonomy. As we progressed in our understanding of the private system, it became clear, to us at least, that the generation and transmission assets of the client could, with a "little" reorganization, produce a steady income stream and be of considerable interest to longer term investors. Private infrastructure as a separate investible asset class was relatively uncommon in Canada at the time, but it was slowly making a comeback.

Enthused by this possibility, our client presentation quickly sped through the relatively routine and mundane matter for which we had been invited. Instead, I spent most of our allotted time on the unique features of the power assets of the company and suggested that they be spun off through an initial public offering (IPO) and listed on the Toronto Stock Exchange (TSE). Although the company's evaluating team politely listened to the thirty-minute presentation, the presentation was deemed unresponsive, and we were not retained for the HQ matter. It was understandable. We had given short shrift to the mission at hand and strayed from our legal lane into a more business-oriented one. I was nonetheless disappointed that the spinoff idea had not generated more curiosity and returned to my work in Canada and abroad. About two months later, while in India on a file, I received a phone call in the middle of the night from my office advising me that the company wanted to further explore the idea of the spinoff.

Upon my return, a team was formed, and meetings were organized. The first order of the day was to examine what was required to carry out the spinoff and how to do it efficiently. One of SE's more creative tax partners agreed to join the team. After a little while, and many questions answered, he asked whether the spin off could be made using a trust formed under the laws of Quebec. It would be a novel structure. I did not see any impediment. He was particularly interested in a feature of Quebec trusts: *le patrimoine d'affectation.* Unlike common law trusts, Quebec law provides that trusts have a patrimony that may be considered theirs. That feature was very relevant for tax purposes, including obtaining the all-important advanced tax ruling from the federal tax authorities confirming the tax benefits of the proposed trust structure.

In 1999, after eighteen months of work, the last permits and approvals having been obtained and the advanced tax ruling having been received, the income trust was created, the spinoff was carried out, and the trust units were listed on the TSE.

I am told that "our" business income trust was a first in Canadian financial circles. The income trust model up to that time had been used as a tax flow through mechanism in connection with extractive industries and real estate, and not with active businesses. As a result, SE had first mover advantage, and our business income trust could serve as a model for the conversion of corporations into income trusts.

The structure was so popular, in fact, that the Government of Canada on October 31, 2006, made the unexpected announcement that as of December 31, 2006, all business income trusts domiciled in Canada would be taxed like corporations, effectively removing the main benefit of income trusts. The main advantage of a business income trust was that its net income could be taxed in the hands of the unit holders rather than the trust, provided that certain conditions were met.

There were serious concerns in Ottawa that the business income trust structure was materially eroding the tax base of the federal and provincial governments, and it was deemed imperative to put an early end to the structure. At the time, there were more than 250 income trusts of all kinds listed on the TSE, and many more were being planned. The market capitalization of income trusts in 2000 on the TSE was approximately C$18 billion. By 2004, the market capitalization had grown to approximately C$118 billion and would continue to grow until 2006. Please remember that a billion dollars in those days was still a very large amount of money.

While the team's tax and securities attorneys at the 1999 closing were delighted with the transaction, I was particularly satisfied with the team's early identification of certain risks and their allocation away from our client. If our client had not identified and dealt early with such risks, the transaction would have been greatly delayed. When some parties to the transaction raised concerns late in the day, we were able to refer to the preliminary documentation signed eighteen months prior and end the matter. As any professional will attest, it is very satisfying to have anticipated and dealt with an issue very much in advance.

FIRST MOVER ADVANTAGE

The income trust episode is a clear demonstration of how disparate files can cross-fertilize. There have been many occasions where work abroad gave us first mover advantage domestically. We were working abroad on renewable energy projects long before Quebec launched its first wind power request for proposals in 2003. This allowed SE Montreal to develop a dominant position in that growing sector.

In addition to gaining valuable industry knowledge, our activities abroad allowed us to meet prospective clients before they came to Canada. Spain is a major player when it comes to infrastructure construction and operation. In 2009, Spain was deep into a banking crisis. Its major construction and renewable energy companies were anxiously looking for new markets to compensate for the situation in Spain.

Canada and, to a lesser extent, some US states were starting to implement PPPs and renewable energy projects. The year before, I had represented Macquarie, a very well-known Australian infrastructure specialist, in Quebec's first PPP. Building upon that and other files, Bertrand Ménard, a SE partner, and I flew to Madrid in 2009 for a week and visited Spanish clients and cold-called others in the Spanish infrastructure and renewable energy space. Our timing could not have been better: Within months, many of these same Spanish companies were looking at entering the Canadian market, and we were only happy to assist.

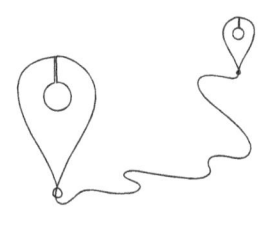

CHAPTER SEVEN

SHARING

Canada's population broke the forty million mark in 2023. According to the 2021 census, about 23 percent of Canada's population is foreign-born. Contrast this with about 14 percent in the US. In many Canadian metropolitan areas, the percentage is much higher. In 2022, Canada admitted over 430,000 immigrants. Canada's constitution recognizes that its founding peoples are the Indigenous Peoples (First Nations, Inuit, and Métis), French Canadians, and English Canadians.

Canada also acknowledges that while most Canadians issue from the founding peoples, Canada has greatly benefited from immigration. Traditionally, most immigrants came from Europe. Now, they come mostly from Asia. In 2022, the top five sources of immigrants to Canada were India, China, Afghanistan, Nigeria, and the Philippines. France was a distant sixth. As a result, Canada is not only an immigrant country, but home to an increasingly multicultural population.

While multiculturalism is generally accepted as a good thing in English Canada, the same is not necessarily true among French Canadians. For many, multiculturalism simply means that the French language and their culture is reduced to being one among many. Francophone Canadians—that is, persons whose first language at home is French—represent more than 80 percent of the population of Quebec, Canada's second largest province, but only about 21 percent of Canada's population.

There is a concern among many francophone Canadians that multiculturalism will have the effect of drowning the French language and the francophone cultures of Canada into some sort of English-speaking melting pot. In Quebec, the law recognizes French as the sole official language, and Quebec exercises some control over immigration. At the Canadian federal level and in the province of New Brunswick, the French language is recognized with English as one of two official languages.

Many Indigenous Peoples also have linguistic and cultural concerns. Demographic growth in Canada continues to be primarily from immigration. How Canada reconciles the need to create an inclusive environment for its ever-growing number of newcomers with the concerns of its French-speakers and Indigenous Peoples may very well determine whether Canada remains unified. The good thing here is that Canada is generally open to doing better and understands that failure threatens its continued existence. As one future federal minister of justice of Canada once told me during a Montreal Canadiens hockey game: "While Canada is probably the best country to be discriminated in, this is by no means satisfactory, and we must do better."

During my four decades on the road, I repeatedly heard development specialists attribute many economic and social development challenges to the fact that the international borders of many countries had arbitrarily been determined by conquest, treaty, or ease of administration. Their populations were ethnic and cultural mosaics with little shared history. These specialists held the firm view that countries do better when they have relatively homogeneous populations.

As a Canadian, I am not sure that I accept this point of view, but I acknowledge that multiculturalism is difficult to master. It requires constant effort on the part of the authorities and populations. It is so transformative that many countries resist it completely.

France refuses multiculturalism and effectively promotes "assimilation" in public life. In the name of "Republican values," France is officially inattentive to ethnicity and authorities collect little data on the subject. France can only guess the size, location, or socioeconomic data of its minorities, whether they be North African, sub-Saharan African, or from another region. To date, the "French way" has produced very uncertain results.

Japan has, for much of its recent history, rejected immigration at scale and perforce multiculturalism. In fact, Japan was essentially a closed country until the Meiji Restoration in the second half of the nineteenth century. As a result, it has by far the most homogeneous population of the G7. But this comes at quite a price. Japan's population is old, resulting in a considerable burden on its younger generations. For decades, starting in the early 1980s, Japan has poured large amounts of money in robotics and artificial intelligence in the hope of compensating for its lack of demographic growth. The results are mixed, if not underwhelming. Without a change in its approach, Japan's population will continue to rapidly decrease. According to the Statistics Bureau of Japan, Japan's population as of October 2022 was approximately 125 million. Japan's National Institute of Population and Social Security Research estimates that Japan's population will fall to about 100 million in 2050 and continue to decline thereafter.

Why do some multicultural countries do better than others? In my experience, it is because they share wealth equitably or at least strive to do so. Yes, over time, equitable wealth sharing is not enough and other steps are required, but it is the bedrock on which successful multicultural societies can exist and thrive. Equal per capita government spending sends a very tangible and powerful message that everyone is valued equally, at least in the eyes of the authorities.

BOTSWANA

Sometimes a jurisdiction will surprise because it does not make headlines and quietly goes about its business.

In 2000, SE won a competitive process to assist IFC on an interesting aviation mandate. Botswana was looking to privatize Air Botswana, its small national airline. The aircraft fleet consisted primarily of three leased ATR 42. The ATR 42 is a French Italian twin turboprop passenger aircraft jointly developed by Aerospatiale (now part of Airbus) and Aeritalia (now Leonardo). The mandate came on the heels of a sad event that occurred the year before.

Before 6:00 a.m. on October 11, 1999, a captain from Air Botswana walked onto the tarmac at Gaborone's Sir

Seretse Khama International Airport, boarded an empty ATR 42, started its engines, and took off—all without any permission whatsoever. The airport was deserted, and the control tower was empty. The captain had been grounded after failing a physical—a decision that did not sit well with him. He proceeded to circle the airport while threatening to crash into the head office of the airline. When he was told it was not empty, he backtracked, demanding to speak to numerous individuals, including the vice-president of Botswana.

After two hours, and running low on fuel, the pilot agreed to land and surrender to the authorities. He landed safely, but instead of slowly proceeding to the terminal, he rammed Air Botswana's two other ATR 42 at more than two hundred knots. The three planes exploded and were destroyed. The pilot was the only casualty. Air Botswana's entire fleet had been destroyed in one event. Two of the planes were the property of the airline, and one had been leased from the manufacturer. The airline's insurer indemnified Air Botswana. The airline promptly leased three new ATRs and banked the insurance proceeds. According to local media, the captain had recently been diagnosed with AIDS.

Botswana is a landlocked country the size of France. It has borders with South Africa, Namibia, Zambia, and Zimbabwe. It has a small population of under 2.5 million and is statistically considered an upper middle-income country. Of course, there are income disparities that are unfortunately widening, and the increase in youth unemployment is an issue. But because of its track record of continuity, peacefulness, fiscal discipline, long-term policies, relatively low corruption, and economic good management, Botswana is often held out as a model for other sub-Saharan countries.

The US, in particular, has developed a good relationship with Botswana, and many US elected officials make a point of visiting the country when in office, including presidents Clinton and G. W. Bush. As a result, Botswana can punch above its demographic and economic weight in regional diplomatic matters.

Botswana's previous name was Bechuanaland. It became a British protectorate in 1885 primarily to prevent Boers and thereafter South Africa from annexing it. Botswana's small and relatively pleasant capital, Gaborone or Gabs for short, feels a world away from Johannesburg, but is only five hours away by car. During Apartheid, many of the world's biggest names in rock music held large outdoor concerts in Gabs so they could cater to their mostly white fans in South Africa without appearing to support the white South African regime by breaking international sanctions against the Pretoria regime.

The national flag is another indication of Botswana's exceptionalism. There are fifty-five member states in the African Union, and Botswana is one of two states — the other being Somalia — that does not incorporate red, green, or yellow/gold in its flag. These are the three colours of the Pan-African flag.

The Botswana flag was created at the time of independence in 1966, in part in opposition to the South African flag. It has three colours: light blue to represent water and its importance (much of Botswana is arid or desert) and black and white to emphasize harmony among races, as well as to represent the zebra, the country's national animal. There never was a large white population in the country for the simple reason that Botswana was unsuited to agriculture and, as such, was of little importance to outsiders during colonization.

About 3 percent of the population is of European descent. It is, therefore, all the more remarkable that such small group would be represented in the flag, unless one romantically takes into account the fact the first lady of Botswana at the time of independence was a white woman from South London whose story is told in the 2016 movie *A United Kingdom*.

The economy of Botswana is relatively well run, and its principal exports include diamonds, copper, gold, and cattle. In addition, Botswana actively protects about 20 percent of its territory and has developed a successful low-impact tourism industry. According to the International Monetary Fund (IMF), Botswana's currency reserves at the end of 2022 provided coverage of nearly seven months of imports. Seven months of import coverage generally demonstrates disciplined economic management and is considered advantageous. In 2000, the import coverage was twenty-five months. I remember at the time that the IMF had the pleasant and rather welcomed task of trying to convince the government to spend more.

Botswana continues to suffer greatly from HIV and AIDS. In 2022, it had one of the world's highest occurrence rates. It was the same during our mandate, the difference being that at this time, the mortality rate from the disease has greatly decreased thanks to improved treatments and government medical expenditures. Contrary to many countries in sub-Saharan Africa, Botswana did not try for religious, ethnic, or domestic political reasons to downplay or hide the crisis. This was and remains in sharp contrast with what other countries in the region have done.

Botswana is often referred to as an ethnically homogeneous country, and at first glance, it appears so. But it would be more appropriate to refer to it as a country with a dominant ethnic group that includes a few smaller ethnic groups. Nearly 80 percent of the population belongs to the dominant Setswana-speaking tribes. A large dominant ethnic group often discriminates against smaller ethnic groups, and this, in turn, creates friction and eventually conflict. How has Botswana been able to avoid this curse and be one of the most peaceful countries in Africa? It seems it is a combination of good fortune, good early leaders, and the relatively equitable and effective expenditure of precious government revenues.

The good fortune came six months after independence when the first large diamond mine was discovered in 1967 by a team of De Beers geologists. Following the discovery, Debswana Diamond Company (Pty) Limited (Debswana), a 50/50 joint venture, was formed between the government of Botswana and De Beers in 1969, and the Orapa mine was opened in 1971. Since then, Debswana has opened three other mines. In 2022, Debswana was the world's leading diamond producer by value. Botswana's early leaders showed considerable foresight by causing Botswana to retain partial ownership of the mines. The revenues from Debswana have given much needed financial resources to the government.

The government has managed its revenues more wisely than most countries and perhaps nowhere more so than in education. At independence in 1966, Botswana had relatively few schools and a very low literacy rate, even by African standards. School curricula were basic, and there were no tertiary institutions. The government has focused on education for all by greatly improving the educational infrastructure everywhere in the country, facilitating attendance, creating better adapted curricula, and developing tertiary education facilities. As a result, Botswana today has one of the highest literacy rates in Africa.

Like all countries, Botswana is not perfect and faces many challenges, including the need to diversify its economy away from mining and increase opportunity for its youth. Nonetheless, the relatively equitable expenditure of government revenues on education and other social programs has enabled the country to execute on the vision of its leaders at the time of independence and become one of Africa's success stories.

CANADA

Canada is another example of a former colony that is multicultural and where sharing government wealth is one of the basic pillars on which the country is built. The Constitution Act (1982) provides at subsection 36(2) that "Parliament and the government of Canada are committed to the principle of making equalization payments to ensure that provincial governments have sufficient funds to provide reasonably comparable public levels of services at reasonably comparable levels of taxation."

The current equalization payment system has been in place since 1957. Canada has ten provinces, and all of them have at one time or another benefited from equalization, but none more than Quebec, at least in absolute terms. Deciding how to spend federal government revenues has been a subject of much debate since the birth of the Canadian Confederation on July 1, 1867. But the subject of late has become more contentious. Because the calculation methodology used to determine such payments is hard to put into sound bites, the issue is susceptible to much distortion, and politicians on both sides of the issue have obliged. The fact that Quebec is a primary beneficiary of the system further complicates the discussion as resentment toward Quebec's francophone identity may be exacerbating the debate in certain circles.

The charge for change in equalization payments is led by Alberta, the most fiscally conservative and richest province, per capita. Alberta is a major oil and gas producer. Hydrocarbons are Canada's number one export by value, with nearly all exports going to the US. Because of its geographical location north of Montana, and its strong oil and gas links to Texas, Alberta often looks to the US for policy inspiration. Quebec, on the other hand, looks to Scandinavia, and to a lesser degree France, for social policy ideas.

Should the equalization payment debate escalate, and a consensus develop in English Canada for changes to the system that are unacceptable to Quebec, it is unlikely that Canada would survive in its current form, and Quebec would most probably go its own way. When discussing equalization, some English Canadians accuse Quebec of being in confederation only for the money. Without considering the merits of that argument, imagine what refusing to share says to a resident of Quebec and such resident's worth within Canada. South African diplomats would run around Tokyo in the 1980s telling anyone who would listen that South Africa spent more per capita on social programs on its various populations than any other country in Africa. The problem, of course, was that whatever it spent on whites was substantially higher per capita than whatever it spent on non-white ethnicities. Canada would be sending a similar message, one that it sent for decades to the Indigenous Peoples in Canada with regrettable consequences.

CHAPTER EIGHT

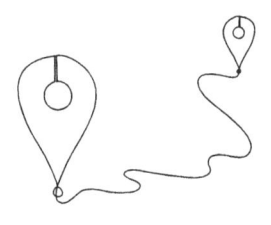

ALL POLITICS IS LOCAL

Tip O'Neill, the powerful Democratic Speaker of the US House of Representatives from 1977 to 1987 and US representative for North Boston from 1953 to 1987, is closely associated with the phrase "all politics is local." Putting this motto into practice with much vigour and enthusiasm, perhaps nowhere more so than in connection with Boston's Big Dig, he was re-elected sixteen times. Big Dig is the nickname given to a series of mega road and tunnel projects planned from 1982 and built between 1991 and 2006 that transformed Boston. Upon O'Neill's death in 1993, President Clinton said that he "was the nation's most prominent, powerful, and loyal champion of working people."

It is now a widely accepted good practice in much of the world that when undertaking a natural resource, infrastructure, or other disruptive project for the benefit of faraway populations or industry, the promoters should provide some direct benefit to the communities surrounding the project. This is particularly true in jurisdictions where government is unable or unwilling to provide basic social services and infrastructure. Expressed in its simplest form, if one builds a hydroelectric plant in a region without power for the benefit of distant load centres, the promoter should make sure to, at the very least, provide power for the surrounding communities.

This commonsense approach, however, is inconsistently applied in wealthier nations where the rule of law and the provident state have, in the minds of promoters, reduced or eliminated the need for a direct beneficial link between a project and local communities, leaving it to the state to provide whatever is needed. This line of thinking is problematical as overreliance on the legal right to do something combined with few, if any, direct local benefits may imperil otherwise perfectly sound projects. Such overreliance usually results in the promoters wasting precious time trying to get complicated legal and technical messages across, instead of plainly addressing the wants and needs of those immediately affected by a given project. In other words, when trying to obtain community support, time is of the essence.

In 2015, I was invited to sit on a panel in Calgary regarding a major oil pipeline project that would cross Quebec. When asked what the sponsors of the project should do to secure Quebec's approval, I blurted that they should seduce Quebec communities along the way. The room appeared both amused and somewhat shocked by the statement, particularly as it was coming from a lawyer. Perhaps the comment would have come across better in French, but what I meant was that the sponsors should waste no time making their projects directly relevant to local communities, rather than relying on their legal rights and appearing to share as little as possible.

☙

I have also applied O'Neill's phrase when trying to figure out why an individual is for or against something. Often, the individual will couch their position in high-minded language when in fact the reasons are more prosaic and often personal. It is one of the reasons why negotiators try to get to know each other to better understand what makes them tick. It's not always easy to do when confronted with language and culture barriers, so in such moments, the assistance of someone with deep local knowledge is essential.

US-CANADA POWER TRANSMISSION LINES

In the early 2010s, I worked on the Quebec side of the Northern Pass power transmission project. The project was to bring "green" Quebec hydroelectric electricity to Massachusetts via New Hampshire. Shortly after it was announced, local opposition in northern New Hampshire coalesced and challenged the project. Apparently, not everyone in New Hampshire thought that allowing high-voltage power lines to cross their state to serve the needs of prosperous Boston was a good thing, per se. In their opinion, there was little direct benefit for the communities along the power line route and much inconvenience.

Opposition continued to grow, even after the promoters offered to bury at considerable cost substantial portions of the line and otherwise reduce the visual and other impacts of the project. With the project being greatly delayed, and opposition becoming intransigent, the project was abandoned in December 2019. For many, climate change remains a remote concern, and the green credentials of hydropower are insufficient to quiet their opposition to high-voltage transmission lines crossing their forests and valleys.

A similar result was narrowly avoided in connection with the New England Clean Energy Connect (NECEC), a US$1 billion 1,200 MW transmission project from Quebec to Massachusetts by way of Lewiston, Maine. As with the Northern Pass project, the objective was to transport hydroelectricity purchased from HQ to Boston. Although most of the electricity will be consumed in Massachusetts, Maine is guaranteed 500,000 MWh per year for twenty years as an incentive to allow the NECEC to traverse the state.

This is all very nice, but the politics of rural and blue-collar resentment and grievance nearly scuttled the NECEC. The project runs through Maine's second US congressional district. This district, which covers much of Maine and is one of the most rural in the US, gave both its popular and electoral college vote to President Trump in the 2016 and 2020 elections. In fact, the pro-Trump vote increased in 2020. Like Nebraska, Maine does not allocate all of its presidential electoral votes to the winner of the state's popular vote, and President Trump won the electoral college vote attached to Maine's second US congressional district.

On January 15, 2020, NECEC's sponsors, including HQ, publicly confirmed that after a lengthy process lasting nearly three years, the NECEC had secured all major state and federal permits and was now "shovel-ready." Ordinarily, this milestone would mark the beginning of the construction phase. Apparently not in Maine, however. On January 15, 2021, the US Court of Appeals in Boston issued an injunction suspending work on the Forks-to-Quebec section of the project. Work in that section required the clearing of a new right of way. In a concession to opponents, the right of way was narrower than usual, thus substantially reducing the environmental footprint of the new build. Environmental groups were challenging whether one of the federal permits was properly issued.

In addition, on January 21, 2021, a coalition of groups opposed to the NECEC delivered a petition with one hundred thousand signatures to the Maine secretary of state. The petition asked that the secretary of state place a citizens' initiative on the November ballot that would, among other things, retroactively require state legislature approval for transmission lines over fifty miles long and prohibit power line construction in the Upper Kennebec region; thus, in effect, terminating the NECEC.

Opponents of the transmission project were a broad coalition that included rural populations, hunters, national environmental groups, Indigenous peoples, and incumbent electricity companies with deep pockets and a willingness to spend. On November 2, 2021, the state of Maine carried out the referendum. At the time, Maine had a population of just under 1.4 million. A little more than four hundred thousand Mainers voted on the referendum, with 60 percent rejecting the NECEC. In other words, only 40 percent of voters supported the project.

Depending on the opponent, one of three arguments was given: (i) opposition to the construction of the Forks-to-Quebec portion as it would encroach on wilderness; (ii) dissatisfaction with, and distrust of, the local power company, Central Maine Power, a major proponent of the

NECEC; and (iii) competition with present and future local electricity producers. The opposition was well funded and had "lawyered up" with a communication strategy that reached far beyond New England.

Tucker Carlson, the TV commentator of Vladimir Putin interview fame, jumped into the fray in late April 2021. His piece on Fox Nation decried the environmental damage being caused by foreign companies in what he described as the "largest forest" in the US Northeast.

How do you compensate a population for crossing their territory? In my opinion, the answer is relatively simple: by doing so as directly and immediately as possible. Payments and power for the state of Maine and the green benefits were distant and intangible in the minds of many project opponents. The fact that the project proponents made derogatory statements about the good faith of the opponents and the quality of their arguments only further fuelled opposition.

In an HBO Axios interview that aired on May 7, 2021, Senator Bernie Sanders from neighbouring Vermont was asked why the Democratic Party has had such a hard time with rural and non-college voters. Senator Sander's answer was straightforward: The Democratic Party has focused on urban and college-educated voters and ignored rural and non-college-educated voters and their concerns. Moreover, the attitude of the Democratic Party and its wealthy coastal backers has been condescending and arrogant. This behaviour created a vacuum and allowed the Republican Party to step in and amplify rural and blue-collar resentment and grievances.

In August 2022, the Supreme Judicial Court of Maine determined that the law passed in the November 21, 2021 referendum was unconstitutional. In April 2023, the

Superior Court of Maine finally gave the green light to the project. Construction of the project resumed in the summer of 2023.

ENERGY EAST OIL PIPELINE

In October 2014, TransCanada Pipelines, a Calgary-based publicly listed corporation, filed a formal proposal with Canada's National Energy Board for a 4,600 km oil pipeline linking Alberta to the East Coast of Canada. The primary purpose of the pipeline was to facilitate the export of Alberta and Dakota oil to new markets through the port of Saint John, New Brunswick, and possibly a port in Quebec. The then-CEO of HQ qualified the project as pharaonic and doubted it would ever be built. Once commissioned, the pipeline would be the longest in North America and cross hundreds of bodies of water, both large and small. Oil pipelines were already present in Ontario and Quebec, but they primarily served the needs of the two provinces. Export oil did travel by rail through both provinces on its way to the Atlantic coast, but did so stealthily until the tragedy of July 6, 2013, when a train carrying oil exploded in the middle of the night in the small Quebec town of Lac-Mégantic, killing forty-seven persons. The blast area extended one kilometre from its epicentre. Although not its primary purpose, one benefit of the Energy East pipeline would be an end to rail transport, a means of transportation that is statistically far more dangerous to humans and the environment than pipelines.

Energy East, due to its interprovincial character, fell primarily under the jurisdiction of the federal government of Canada, but politics made it a sine qua non that the pipeline be acceptable to the provinces it would traverse.

New Brunswick, the intended home of the Saint John pipeline terminal, was very much in favour. On the other hand, Ontario and Quebec, home to more than 50 percent of Canada's population, were skeptical, with the two provinces jointly adopting a list of conditions that the project would have to satisfy. The conditions were comprehensive, unsurprising, and probably doable. One of the conditions, of course, made provision for local acceptance and benefits.

Unfortunately for Energy East, its proponents placed much reliance, at least at first, on their legal rights and less on social acceptability and other softer considerations. This meant that the promoters lost precious time developing a compelling case. This allowed pipeline opposition to organize and, with time, harden to a point where compromise became difficult and synonymous with capitulation.

The fact that the pipeline opposition seemed to be constantly moving the goal posts, ensuring that the proponents appeared one step behind, did not help. The pipeline was formerly cancelled in October 2017. In hindsight, this may have been a blessing in disguise if one looks at the travails and massive cost overruns encountered by another pipeline: the Trans Mountain Expansion project, a 980 km oil pipeline that runs from Alberta to Burnaby on the British Columbia Pacific coast. That pipeline was completed in the first half of 2024.

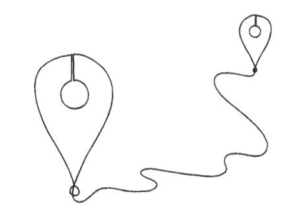

CHAPTER NINE

GREAT GAME

Over the course of my practice, the superpower world changed on two occasions. During the Cold War, which ended in 1991 with the dissolution of the USSR, it was a two-superpower world with the US and the USSR facing each other and acting through proxies. Many countries were aligned with one side or the other. Others belonged to the Non-Aligned Movement, but the movement's more important members each had their preferred camp.

When you arrived in a country during the Cold War, knowing the extent to which the country belonged or leaned toward one of the two geopolitical camps was a must. It helped to understand and predict how the authorities approached a variety of matters: document drafting, contract sanctity, private ownership, dispute resolution, enforcement of arbitral and judicial awards, access to foreign exchange, and so on.

After 1991 came a period when the US was the only superpower. This period lasted about twenty years and was a time of relative calm. Most countries were moving toward the same goals, many with the help of the IFIs. During this period, there was a more uniform approach to transactions, and the work of negotiators was made easier.

With the economic and military rise of China, we are now effectively back to a two-superpower world. The world is more turbulent, and political risks are on the rise. Lesser actors, Russia first among them, are acting out, often with the tacit or express consent of one of the superpowers. Smaller countries are offering to the highest bidder their allegiance and sometimes more. The Solomon Islands, a country where Massicotte did some work privatizing SOEs in the '00s, signed a security agreement with China in 2022. It allows China's navy the right to dock and replenish in that country. China will no doubt try to do the same thing over time with other Pacific island nations. This development is unnerving the US and Australia as the security agreement places a growing Chinese blue water navy near sea lanes between the two countries.

In a two-superpower world, it is very difficult to remain neutral and still benefit from superpower protection. One small country in the Horn of Africa is trying to be one of the few exceptions to the general rule. That country is Djibouti. I came to know Djibouti while working there on a strategically important transaction in 2012–2013.

DJIBOUTI

Djibouti, a country with a little more than one million inhabitants, surrounds a large deep water natural bay located at the mouth of the Red Sea, opposite Yemen. The country occupies only 23,200 km², an area slightly smaller than the US state of Vermont. Djibouti is ill-suited for agriculture, but does have a number of geological marvels, including Lake Assal, considered by some to be the world's largest salt reserve. Lake Assal is also the world's third lowest point at 155 m below sea level. The first and second lowest points being the Sea of Galilee and the Dead Sea.

France's colonization of Djibouti began in 1884. By 1960, all but two of France's sub-Saharan overseas territories had gained independence. Djibouti was one of the two exceptions, the other being the Comoros, which gained its independence in 1975. Djibouti remained a French overseas territory until 1977, when it became independent. In 1967, its name was changed from French Somalia to Territoire français des Afars et des Issas, referencing the two main ethnic groups of Djibouti. The Issa, in fact, speak Somali and fluidly move across the border with Somaliland.

Djibouti is surrounded by turbulent and far more populous countries: Somaliland to the south, Ethiopia to the west, Eritrea to the north and Yemen across the Bab-el-Mandeb Strait (Gate of Tears).

Somaliland is the northern most province of Somalia and since 1991, functions as a de facto country. Until 1960, Somaliland was a British protectorate known as British Somalia. Four days after its 1960 independence, it joined the former Italian Somaliland to form Somalia. Both Somalia and, more threateningly, Ethiopia, a landlocked country with a population of more than 120 million beset periodically by hunger and civil unrest — if not civil war — have historically claimed Djibouti.

Ethiopia's Western-leaning Emperor Haile Selassie, a Christian as well as a religious figure among some Rastafarians, was overthrown in 1974 and replaced by the Derg military council, a very harsh regime. In 1977, Ethiopia aligned with the USSR and its allies to defend against Somalia's planned invasion and annexation of the Ogaden, a province of Ethiopia. At the time, Ethiopia was in the grip of considerable internal unrest, including along its Eritrean coastline.

Somalia launched its invasion in July 1977, only to be eventually beaten back by Ethiopia with the help of more than twelve thousand Cuban troops, fifteen hundred Soviet advisers, and a massive airlift of materiel and munitions. The war lasted eight months. The Cuban troops were instrumental in winning the war and remained in Ethiopia until 1989, when Ethiopia and Somalia formally agreed to recognize their borders.

During the 1980s, the Cold War was alive and well in the Horn of Africa with Cuban soldiers staring across the border at elements of the French Foreign Legion stationed in Djibouti. The legion left its permanent Djibouti base in 2011, but other French forces remain, and Djibouti is home to France's largest military installations in Africa.

Djibouti currently has two main economic activities: (i) it is the main gateway to Ethiopia and, to a lesser extent, South Sudan, and (ii) it hosts a number of foreign military bases.

In 2023, more than 95 percent of Ethiopia's trade by volume was transported on the Addis Ababa-Djibouti corridor, mostly by truck. Every day, long columns of trucks patiently wait to load or unload at Djibouti's port and slowly return to Ethiopia. The road needs much repair and is congested.

To provide congestion relief and redundancy, the Addis Ababa–Djibouti Railway was built and financed by Chinese concerns and commenced operations on January

1, 2018. The railroad is owned by a joint venture between the Ethiopian and Djibouti governments and carries both cargo and passengers. Because it opened before completion of the supporting infrastructure, it has not yet reached its full potential. In the meantime, this railroad has saddled Ethiopia and Djibouti with much debt and could serve as a case study for the risks posed by poor project conception.

Djibouti is also a permanent base and port of call for many armed forces. The bases do not all have the same purpose. After 9/11, the US took over Camp Lemonnier, a former French base next to the Djibouti City airport. It serves as the main counterinsurgency base for the US in the region. Drones and other aircraft, both fixed winged and rotary, regularly take off from there. It also serves as an important base in the fight against piracy in the Gulf of Aden and the Indian Ocean.

Japan has a base in Djibouti, its first semi-permanent foreign base, ostensibly to help in the fight against piracy. Italy has a support base there, and other countries, including Germany, Spain, and Sweden, have sent military and police personnel to assist with anti-piracy efforts.

Many of the countries that send personnel to Djibouti have them stay on the US or French bases or in the hotels in Djibouti City that meet international standards. In the early 2010s, there were two such hotels—the Kempinsky being the hotel of choice. Because of the risk of car bombings, taxis and most civilian vehicles could not enter the hotel perimeter, and guests had to walk the last one hundred or so metres with their luggage in tow. It made everybody look like they were headed to an Airbnb. The precautions were not in vain, however. Terrorist attacks, although rare, were a very possible occurrence. One restaurant we frequented was bombed with loss of life three weeks after our last visit there.

Djibouti is also home to China's first overseas military base. The base was inaugurated on August 1, 2017. It has expanded since. It is located only a few kilometres from the US base, the French air base, and the Japanese base. When it was first announced, it caused considerable consternation among the other foreign forces, particularly the US and Japanese. The US went so far as to say they felt blindsided by Djibouti. The response of Djibouti was essentially to tell everyone to chill and play nice.

But unlike the other foreign powers, China has not just built a base. It has bought participations in Djibouti's infrastructure and lent large sums in the furtherance of Djibouti's economic development. As a result, Djibouti is highly indebted to China. This has the danger of disturbing the uneasy equilibrium in Djibouti between the two superpowers and their allies.

One consequence of Djibouti's strategy, intended or not, has been to insulate the government from much foreign criticism and pressure, with neither superpower being interested in antagonizing its landlord. As a result, private investors in Djibouti must carefully weigh the novel risks posed by a small country playing both sides of the geopolitical divide. The Doraleh Container Terminal dispute pitting Djibouti against the UAE is a very informative case study in this regard.

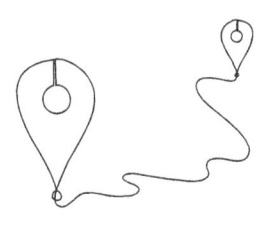

CHAPTER TEN

INDIA

India will, in the longer term, be the most consequential country where we worked. Our team completed mandates in approximately ten Indian states, including Gujarat, Prime Minister Modi's home state, where it was crystal clear that efficiency was high up on the list of priorities. We started shortly after the July 1991 historic budget of then minister of finance Dr. Singh and continued into the early 2000s. Our clients were state governments and SEBs in need of assistance in reforming their electricity sectors or in dealing with IPPs. Some of the mandates were led by my partners Martin Scheim and Christine Desaulniers, others by me.

1991 SINGH BUDGET

The 1991 Central Government budget tabled by Dr. Singh broke with the past and introduced a number of path-breaking economic reforms to reduce the economic role of the state and move to an economy led by the private sector.

The first reform began with the budget chipping away at the "License Raj." This less-than-flattering phrase refers to the bureaucracy that commands and controls large swaths of the Indian economy through its onerous and sometimes controversial and ethically challenging licensing and permitting system. The budget reduced the number of sectors subject to the full attention of the License Raj and made it easier to start and expand a business.

The second reform encouraged foreign direct investment into India, a country whose economy was effectively closed to foreigners for most of the post-independence period when India was following an economic model based in part on Fabian socialism and whose investment climate was deemed too time consuming and ethically challenging.

In the third reform, the budget sought to privatize some SOEs and allow the private sector, domestic and foreign, to invest in areas that had been the preserve of the state. The electricity sector was one area targeted by the Central Government. The SEBs would not be privatized, but the private sector was welcome to build power plants and sell electricity to the SEBs. In the late 1980s, it became clear that the Indian economy would be constrained by a lack of reliable power unless change came at the state level. The production of electricity was the affair of both the central and state governments. The Central Government had a relatively small number of power plants and electrical transmission lines, including nuclear power plants derived from the Canadian CANDU reactor. These facilities were considered in satisfactory operational and financial state. The same could not be said of the electricity production, transmission, and distribution capacity of most SEBs. The number one problem for SEBs being money.

SEBs had serious difficulty collecting accounts receivables from state governments and SOEs. There was also the matter of what is euphemistically called "non-technical losses," the common practice of customers illegally connecting to distribution power lines and not paying for the power so consumed—many such connections being made after working hours by moonlighting employees of the SEBs.

Because of a lack of money, maintenance and repair on the SEB facilities were delayed, leading to less than optimum efficiency. Much of India's electricity was and is produced using Indian coal, whose quality varies depending on the state. To make matters even more challenging, the mining and supply of coal was handled by other SOEs, whose reliability was at times uncertain. All of this to say that the sector at the state level needed much reform, and the Central Government was looking to the private sector for solutions.

As an inducement to private-sector investment, the Central Government gave payment guarantees to eight IPPs. While the offer of such guarantees enticed many to bid for the projects, not all of those that were guaranteed became undeniable successes. One project, the 2,184 MW LNG Dahbol power plant in Bhopal, Maharashtra, was for years the source of many bad headlines around the world, notwithstanding that it had the financial and political backing of the US, including president Clinton. Its principal sponsor, Enron Corporation, went spectacularly bankrupt in 2001 as a result of one of the US's biggest corporate frauds.

More importantly, from an Indian perspective, the agreed contract price for the electricity produced by the plant was unsustainable and had to be renegotiated lest it lead to the eventual bankruptcy of the electricity purchaser, the Maharashtra State Electricity Board. How such a contract was approved by the authorities in the home state of Mumbai, India's financial capital, is somewhat perplexing.

Finally, the budget tackled some fiscal matters: a reduction in import tariffs to expand international trade, a devaluation of the Indian rupee, and measures to reduce fiscal deficits.

India in the 1990s was becoming a two-tracked economy. On one track was the heavily regulated slow-growth older sectors that remained subject to the License Raj. On the other track were newly deregulated sectors and, better still, new and innovative ones that relied on India's human capital and rapid improvements in communications and computing. In 1994, the Central Government opened the telecommunications sector to private long distance, cellular, and internet providers. This deregulation allowed India to become a powerhouse in call centres, back-office processes, and software development. Companies such as Wipro, Infosys, and Tata Communication Services became global players, and Bangalore, Hyderabad, and other cities grew as IT hubs. In 1995, India joined the WTO, further integrating India into the world economy.

OUR WORK

In most of our India files, the frustration of the private-sector participants, whether Indian or foreign, was palpable and difficult to conceal and, to be perfectly frank, totally understandable and justified. Projects were gratuitously taking years to come to fruition and, while doing so, taxing everyone's patience and finances. In most cases, our primary mission was to find ways to secure the electricity purchasing obligations of SEBs and speed things up.

For the most part, the electricity projects were project financed and on a "take or pay" basis. That meant that an SEB was bound to pay a minimum amount even if it did not take any or all of the electricity on offer. This amount had to be sufficient to allow the IPP to pay the project financiers and the operating expenses and allow for a reasonable return for the IPP owners.

Since the root of the SEBs' problems was lack of money, the projects would not be bankable unless the SEBs' payment risk could be mitigated with security and/or credit enhancement. Generally speaking, the only creditworthy guarantor was the Central Government, and New Delhi had made it perfectly clear that it would contractually stand behind only eight IPPs. Outside this golden group of eight, the trick for the SEBs and the IPPs was to cobble together a security package that would satisfy the financiers. In some states, this was possible through complicated escrow schemes and the like.

In the end, our clients were able to close only a few smaller projects that did not necessitate much new infrastructure. These IPPs were power plants with a rated production capacity of 300 MW or less. In some instances, the IPP sponsors were so keen to get into the sector that they were willing to assume risks that would ordinarily be borne by someone else. It was a dangerous thing to do anywhere, India being no exception.

MODI EFFECT

By the late 1990s, the excitement among foreign investors over the Singh budget reforms had dissipated. India has a way of absorbing the impetus for change and, through lethargy, kill innovative ways. India would effectively have to wait until the arrival of Prime Minister Modi in 2014 to rekindle foreign investor excitement. It is, of course, too early to tell whether the "Modi Effect" will last, but there is no denying that India is currently one of the fastest growing major economies and that it has been able to make great economic strides. The fact that developed economies are actively looking to reduce their reliance on China will greatly assist India. India is the most populous country in the world and needs to massively industrialize to provide work and opportunity for its youth.

India makes much of the fact that it is the world's largest democracy, and the country's rule of law is robust. All political systems are flawed to varying degrees, but it is undeniable that Indian democracy exists and that changes in government are made swiftly and generally peacefully, notwithstanding the rough and tumble nature of Indian politics.

As for the rule of law, the most charitable thing I can say is that India in the 1990s and '00s was suffering from too much of a good thing. Laws were often interpreted and applied inconsistently, with frustrating and unfair results. Litigation, or the threat thereof, was used extensively as a negotiating tactic. Courts were extremely slow in rendering decisions, and appeals were frequent. Litigation could remain unresolved for a very long time, and the paralysis that ensued hindered investment and growth despite the obvious opportunities. When Modi first became prime minister, one of his first priorities was the adoption of a modern Insolvency and Bankruptcy Code. Adopted in 2016 the Code essentially provides that deadbeats were now expected to pay, restructure, or disappear with some celerity. Of course, enacting laws is one thing, and enforcing them efficiently is another.

INDIA ADVANTAGES

Many outsiders consider India chaotic and overwhelming. In his seminal work, *India after Gandhi*, Ramachandra Guha writes that the British never believed that India could form one nation. The differences among its various constituent parts were just too great. After all, if Europe with far fewer regional differences could not unite, then how could India with its myriad states—including its more than five hundred princely states immediately before independence—succeed in creating a unified country? India, in Britain's eyes, was a perfect candidate for divide and conquer, and the British succeeded for a while.

Events have proven the British view mostly incorrect even if the creation of India has not been perfect. There were the terrible events in 1947 when India and Pakistan parted ways. There is the continued issue of Kashmir. I have learned from personal experience that the subject is nearly impossible to calmly discuss with Indians or Pakistanis.

There is also episodic sectarian violence, persistent civil unrest in hot spots around India, and, of course, India's abyssal social indicators. India is disproportionately home to many of the world's poorest inhabitants and all of the ills that befall vulnerable populations. India has certainly not lifted out of extreme poverty the incredible numbers that China has. At the beginning of the 1980s, India and China had essentially the same GDP per capita. In 2022, China's GDP per capita was multiples that of India. This has created a geopolitical imbalance that is worrisome for India as the two countries share a long and contested border.

But the GDP of India is now growing faster than that of its rival. China is exiting the economic takeoff phase at the same time that India is now entering it. This high-growth phase is the period when nations grow rapidly because of massive government-led infrastructure and basic industry investments. India has much catching up to do, and it should be one generation before India exits this stage. While many things must fall into place to allow India to catch up, and, in my opinion, eventually surpass China, India has a number of distinct advantages over China.

1. Its demography is favourable in that its population is young and should remain so for a while.

2. English is widely understood and spoken among the educated class.

3. It is geographically well positioned between Europe, Africa, and East Asia.

4. The rule of law prevails over the rule of man despite the efforts of some to subvert this fundamental principle.

5. For all its faults and imperfections, India is a freer country than China. India has a mixed economy with much of it still subject to central or state government controls. But in parallel, there are many sectors of the economy that have been deregulated or are unregulated by default because they are new and there is little

appetite for the authorities to exert any dominion over such sectors. In addition to growing economic freedom, Indians enjoy more personal freedoms than in China. My experience is that once a country has solved its basic needs, it is very difficult to keep the economy growing apace without strong individual freedoms grounded in the rule of law. A more centralized and dirigiste government may be preferable when laying the building blocks of a country, but once that is done, it is preferable to let individuals make the most of such building blocks. It is not enough to have infrastructure, health, and education to ensure success. China is now discovering the complexities of managing an economy that is slowing down and that will need both the private sector and the Chinese consumer to keep growing. Perhaps India's diversity, religiosity, and strong "live and let live" credo have allowed it to develop a freer society.

I will concede, however, that personal freedom is probably a relatively abstract concept to persons who suffer from poverty and a fortiori from extreme poverty. Poverty is a prison, and India, to date, has not equalled the extraordinary poverty eradication success of other countries. Moreover, inequality between urban and rural population is growing and could threaten the cohesion of India and its chances for economic liftoff.

India needs to ensure that its economic prosperity includes and directly benefits rural populations. Rural electrification, inexpensive telephony, easy to use software, the removal from rural life of parasitic middlemen, digital citizen identity, telephone banking, improved sanitation, and many other innovations are all attempts to improve the life of India's rural population. They are also ways in which to build a strong constituency in favour of India's more modern sectors, insulating them from rural resentment and backlash.

CHAPTER ELEVEN

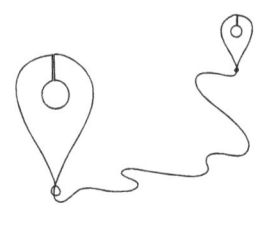

POWER OF THE BRAND

We had two types of clients overseas. The first group included public sector clients: governments, SOEs, and IFIs. The second group was comprised of private-sector corporations and entrepreneurs. The Canadian brand was important with public-sector clients and nearly always irrelevant with private-sector clients.

PUBLIC-SECTOR CLIENTS

I often asked our public-sector clients why we had been hired and most answers centred around the following two themes:

Firstly, Canada is perceived as a middle-sized economic power uninterested in projecting much power beyond its borders. As a percent of GDP, Canada is one of the world's great exporters, but the reach of Canadian corporations and brands rarely extends very far. Whether true or not, we are still viewed as hewers of wood and drawers of water. The beaver is a national symbol of Canada and perfectly reinforces the foreign perception of our national character. We quietly go about building our little pond and appear very content doing so. Since we are not a major international actor, whether diplomatically, militarily, or economically, there are likely to be fewer conflict-of-interest situations, and Canada can act as an honest broker. This perception of Canada is unlikely to change in the future as Canada continues its trajectory toward international irrelevancy. Our defence and foreign aid budgets and policies have been inadequate for decades, and the situation is unlikely to change anytime soon.

Secondly, Canadians are perceived as easier to work with. We are more flexible, less dogmatic, and more affable than the Americans, the English, or the French. We are also viewed as somewhat boring, but that is a different story for some other time. Our English and French cultures are viewed as subsets rather than stand-alone cultures.

Many Canadians are worldwide stars, but that fact is rarely known. Canadians are open to doing things differently if it makes sense. We do not hesitate to borrow means and methods from others and adapt them as necessary — this is particularly true of Quebecers.

Interestingly, the flexibility and affability themes ring less true with regional powers aspiring to bigger things. These countries prefer to deal with senior powers rather than a middling one like Canada. Brazil and Nigeria are two countries where I have experienced this reluctance.

But what about competence? I remember a client survey that was done in the mid-1990s for the account of major law firms in Toronto, including SE. According to the survey, the number one quality that clients sought from lawyers was that they return phone calls. I was shocked. It was not expertise or creativity. It was a very mundane task that I took for granted.

So if that is the case in Toronto, I should not be surprised if competence was rarely mentioned by our foreign clients. However, even if they did not raise the subject, perceived competence did play a role in file acquisitions. If one looks at the sectors where we won mandates, a pattern becomes apparent. We won mostly in the sectors where Canada is perceived as able: mining, oil and gas, forestry, pipelines, railroads, ports, hydroelectricity, power transmission, and air transport. This strength was forged in large part by Canada's geography and geology. It was easier securing work in these fields than in other sectors. We were credible just because we were from Canada.

In the mid-1990s, we were selected to assist Bolivia in the privatization of its tin mines. It was a contentious file as I discovered when I first arrived in tear-gas-filled La Paz. The miners were forcefully displaying their opposition to the privatizations. What struck me at the time was how the government was using the fact that it had hired a Canadian law firm to convey to all concerned that it was serious about the transactions. Ultimately, the privatizations did not go ahead, in part because due diligence teams were being warned before going down into the mines that descent was assured, but ascent was less so.

Perception can be a double-edged sword, as anyone who has been tightly pigeonholed knows all too well. In the entertainment industry, this is typecasting, and it can be difficult to break out of it. Actors guard against it with varying degrees of success.

There is a perfectly normal tendency for individuals to classify and limit themselves to their classification. Most of the time it is not malicious; it is just a shortcut that busy people use to speed up decision making. Sometimes, of course, our non-Canadian competitors would graciously acknowledge that we had relevant expertise while in the same breath constricting the expertise to some esoteric domain irrelevant to the task at hand. It is a way to eliminate competition.

When asked how we developed our foreign practice, I usually give my one-word cocktail party answer: serendipity. Infrequently, my interlocutors are unsatisfied with the brief answer. In such instances, I continue with some version of the following anecdote, which is a variation on the honest broker theme above.

It was the late 1990s. We had just won a call for proposals to represent an SEB in its negotiations with several Indian IPPs. The transactions were between Indians and had no international features. I had flown in that morning from Frankfurt and upon landing, proceeded immediately to the hotel to freshen up. I then took a taxi to the client's head office and, after being ushered into the elevator reserved for executives, arrived at the executive floor. I was then escorted to a room with a round table, a high ceiling, and a slowly turning fan above the table.

The heads of the three divisions of the SEB were seated at the table: member generation, member transmission, and member distribution. Also seated was the most important person in the room, the Indian Administrative Service (IAS) officer deployed to the SEB. He was impeccably dressed in all white. There was one seat empty, and it was for me. This was my first encounter with the client.

I took my seat and, after the usual civilities, asked my hosts why — since they were better educated and smarter than I was — they had called upon a foreign lawyer to deal with the Indian sponsors of IPPs in what are domestic transactions. They all gave me the Indian head bobble and then there was silence. The three members were probably deferring to the IAS officer, and the IAS officer was, I surmise, hoping to learn something from a member's answer.

After about fifteen seconds, the IAS officer broke the silence and said: "Because we do not trust each other." I had my answer and did not ask for any elaboration, and the table quickly proceeded to discuss the status of the various IPPs. Why spoil what seemed a truthful answer with contrived qualifications and insincere backtracking?

I once mentioned the anecdote to an Indian Central Government minister for electricity. He was on an official visit to Canada, and I was attending a reception in his honour. After finishing the anecdote, he asked for the name of the IAS officer. I demurred as I did not want to get the officer in trouble. He responded that on the contrary he wanted to congratulate him!

The IAS is part of the civil service of the Central Government of India. IAS officers work primarily for the Central Government, but may be deployed to states and SOEs. The recruitment process is very selective. Two out of three IAS officers are direct recruits. Direct recruits are those who have successfully passed the relevant written examination and completed the requisite courses. The acceptance rate is infinitesimally small, less than a small fraction of 1 percent.

The IAS is by no means perfect, but one thing is clear: Its officers are bright even if, at times, innovation averse. They remind me of the graduates of France's École nationale d'administration (ENA), an institution that for seventy-five years produced many of France's senior bureaucrats and politicians. French President Emmanuel Macron, over considerable opposition—including from his prime minister—replaced the school in 2021 with L'Institut national du service public in an effort to create a more open and diverse public service. Time will tell whether the replacement, in many respects cosmetic, will produce the desired result.

PRIVATE-SECTOR CLIENTS

Overseas private-sector clients chose us primarily as a result of special situations. The fact that we were Canadian was a non-factor, except in the very notable case of Cuba.

1. **CUBA:** US sanctions against Cuba limited what US law firms could do in that country. This obviously opened the door for us, something that would have been most unlikely without sanctions. Cuba is less than 150 km from the Florida Keys as the crow flies. We took full advantage of the opportunity. For nearly a decade, we advised a myriad of foreign investors looking to invest into Cuba. The companies were established concerns from Europe, South America, and Asia that wanted to engage in just about every sector of Cuba's economy. The work led to a number of interesting moments. Shortly after it became known in some circles that we were regularly involved in Cuba, I started receiving visits from UK and US firms in the business of advising on country risks. The representatives, all charming and capable, were looking for insights on Cuba and a few other countries where we were involved. These visits continued well into the '00s.

Another interesting sideline was the inspection, for a short moment, of garment factories in Cuba. Prospective importers would supply me with questionnaires that were better suited to the sweatshops of Asia and had little relevance in slow-paced, open-aired Cuba. These questionnaires were so disconnected with the Cuban reality that some of the readers would question my objectivity after I had visited the factories and completed the paperwork. One moment I did not appreciate, however, was when the Canadian government for purely political reasons served me with a copy of the Canadian blocking order, reminding me, and indirectly my firm, of my obligation under Canadian law not to cease doing business in Cuba as a result of US pressure.

2. **RELEVANT EXPERIENCE:** We were sometimes recommended by a government to a private-sector party because we had relevant experience, usually gained in a neighbouring country working for a government or a SOE. Most governments welcomed this in the hope that things would go faster thanks to our presence. Unfortunately, because of the propensity for governments to "innovate" by adding or changing features to projects, the speed element was rarely satisfied.

3. **EXISTING CLIENTS:** In a few cases, foreign clients had worked with us in Canada and were of the opinion that we would be a better fit than their usual international counsel. This was particularly true in the 1990s with respect to the privatizations of SOEs and in the 2010s in connection with PPPs.

4. **CANADIAN LAW:** From time to time, a mining company listed on the TSE—wishing to keep legal fees more reasonable than if it hired a US or UK law firm—would recommend to its financiers that they use Canadian attorneys and have the transaction or elements thereof governed by the laws of a Canadian province, nearly always Ontario.

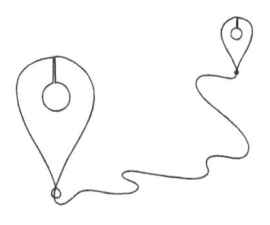

CHAPTER TWELVE

LOCAL KNOWLEDGE, ARTIFICIAL INTELLIGENCE

LOCAL KNOWLEDGE

Adapting expertise to local conditions was essential, and I am thankful that in most jurisdictions we were ably assisted by capable lawyers from first-class local firms. Most lawyers were relatively young and, later in their careers, took full advantage of the opportunities offered to them by their rapidly growing economies. Imagine starting a professional career in an economy that is growing for long periods at a sustained real rate of 5 percent or more per annum.

I learned very quickly that, as in sailing or trekking, local knowledge is essential to get you safely to your destination. Local knowledge is incredibly important for a range of reasons. It allows for improved communications. An understanding of the cultural, social, and historical context is essential to effective communications and developing relationships. It reduces the risk of faux pas, awkward moments, and misunderstandings. Local knowledge is essential to properly structuring projects to ensure a smoother integration into their surroundings. It also allows for better identification and mitigation of local risks, whether commercial or not. This, in turn, can ensure that local concerns, Indigenous practices, traditional wisdom, and local innovations are better taken into account when structuring. All of the above, of course, requires leaving your ego at the airport and being willing to listen and keep an open mind. This is not always easy to do if you are the "expert" from far away, hired at great cost, and everyone is looking at you for immediate solutions.

ARTIFICIAL INTELLIGENCE

In the fall of 2022, Open AI, an American company, released ChatGPT to the public. ChatGPT is a chatbot—that is, a generative artificial intelligence (AI) technology. Unlike the traditional search engines, it produces humanlike responses in seconds or minutes. Open AI's release was done without the fanfare ordinarily associated with Big Tech. This is remarkable considering how this software is world changing. The release of chatbots is being compared to the advent of computers and the internet. In my opinion, it is more important.

Within weeks of the release of ChatGPT, millions of individuals and businesses were testing it and, although it was still a prototype, most were wondrous about its abilities as well as apprehensive about how AI would change their livelihood and business. For the first time, humans have a tool that can assemble data in novel ways and create a finished work, and then build again on such work and repeat the process ad infinitum. In other words, humans have a competitor in the creative space.

This raises many issues, including whether humans will be able to control such technology and whether it will do more harm than good. For the time being, ChatGPT and similar chatbots are imperfect tools that require human input, curation, and verification; however, the day when human intervention is no longer necessary in the creation process is foreseeable. At that point, chatbots could cease to be mere tools and morph into something else.

The fear of computers and AI is not new. Frank Herbert's 1965 novel *Dune* created a world where computers and artificial intelligence had been mostly forbidden following the Butlerian Jihad. This twist in the *Dune* story was useful for storytelling. It also underscores the importance for humans to control the creation and decision-making processes.

AI has many benefits and, as a tool, will accelerate breakthroughs in science and elsewhere. But as with other inventions, it will be misused. The difficulty for humans is that it may be very difficult to know when such misuse is occurring. Deepfakes are already perverting elections. Regulation of AI is obviously required.

Continental Europe will be at the forefront of regulation in much the same way as it currently leads the protection of personal data. As a producer, the Europe Union is a laggard in much of the tech space, but the European Union is the second largest economy in the world, in nominal terms. That simple fact gives it regulatory clout. Moreover, it has a propensity for regulating everything and anything, and the tech lobby in the European Union is nowhere near as large or powerful as in the US.

AI will learn, apply, and expand on many of the lessons mentioned in this book. In the near future, AI will allow negotiating parties to be far better informed and advanced when they first sit down at the negotiating table. This should shorten negotiations. But does that mean that all of the lessons in this book are now irrelevant for humans? I do not think so. In my opinion, it will be a very long time before AI has sufficient emotional intelligence to deal on par with humans. If I am correct and AI, for example, is not able to determine whether a person or group of persons is trustworthy, loyal, honest, truthful, etc., then, a fortiori, delegating the final say in any negotiation to AI would be unwise, and the lessons in this book continue to be relevant for negotiators and advisers.

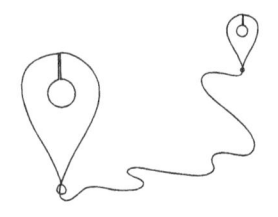

CONCLUSION

The world is full of talented individuals yearning to apply their abilities to the fullest. Unfortunately, many will not be able to do so because of conditions in their home jurisdictions. A few will leave and try to succeed elsewhere, but it will not be easy. It takes a lot of courage to emigrate, whether lawfully or otherwise. I am thankful that this was not my lot. I am fortunate to have been born and raised in countries where you can develop your abilities and apply them.

When I started working abroad, and for some time thereafter, mobile telephony, the internet, and portable computers were not available. On the road, I had to negotiate and draft documents with few, if any, source materials. This forced me to hone my limited analytical and drafting skills. Time spent honing these basic skills gave me an advantage that carried me throughout my career and allowed me to follow economic trends and quickly rotate into new practice sectors.

Many of my private-sector clients were long-standing, with many relationships extending thirty years or more.

My favourite clients were Japanese, and I very much enjoyed working with them. The relationships were less transactional and more human. The close relationship made the work more interesting and allowed for a quick ramp up and efficiency whenever I was called upon to provide services.

The two characters that form the Chinese word for crisis are danger and something akin to opportunity. There have been many crises in countries and regions where I worked and, true to the Chinese word for crisis, they have been sources of opportunity. I have noted a few such crises in this book.

It has been my experience that governments around the world overpromise and underdeliver. This breeds cynicism and frustration. It also results in much waste as limited funds are spread thinly over too many areas, and strained institutional capabilities are unable to cope with surging demand and fail. It also brings forth the scourge of governmental deficits and unsustainable debt.

Canada is not immune to this. We are very far from the 2003 cover of *The Economist* featuring a Canadian moose wearing Oakley glasses. It is time to reorder priorities, concentrate on the feasible, and put the aspirational aside until such time as efficiency and value for money return to government.

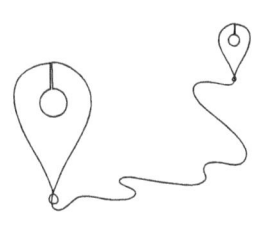

APPENDIX I

COMMERCIAL RISKS

Commercial risks are those operational and financial risks that a project (or business) may encounter while conducting its activities. In this appendix, "project" includes a "business," and the terms are used interchangeably. As a general rule, project participants have primary responsibility for the identification and allocation of commercial risks. Outside consultants, including lawyers, are rarely consulted in connection with risks encountered regularly by their client and within the client's sphere of competence. Nonetheless, and at the risk of being mildly annoying, it is recommended that consultants broach the subject with the client early in the transaction. The simplest way to do this is by means of a matrix with two columns. The first describes each major risk. The second column names the party to whom the risk is usually allocated. The matrix could also include another column very briefly describing the main mitigation strategies, but it is not recommended to burden the document, at least not at the time of its first use with the client.

Generally, long-duration transactions share the following commercial risks:

DEMAND

Demand risk refers to the uncertainties posed by changes in demand for the goods and services of a project. Many projects are predicated upon a minimum product or service demand, failing which the project will not generate sufficient revenues to service its debt, meet its costs, and provide a reasonable return to equity providers. Factors that may impact demand are numerous and include:

THE STATE OF THE ECONOMY. Macro-economic factors will materially affect demand. These include higher interest rates, currency devaluations, inflation, increased unemployment, and population migrations. The US economy is built on consumption financed with credit. In the 2010s, interest rates were so low and lending criteria so generous that consumers and corporations benefited from the equivalent of quasi "free money," and many consumers and corporations made poor choices. Should interest rates return to their historical levels or higher and remain there, consumers and corporations will eventually reduce consumption and investment, with some unable to meet their liabilities as they become due and going bankrupt.

The massive over construction in the residential real estate market in China is another example of the consequences of poor macroeconomics. True statistics are sometimes difficult to come by in China, but it is conservatively estimated that at the end of 2023, there were more than ninety million empty and often unfinished residential dwellings in China. Many, if not most, will never be completed, and they will eventually have to be demolished. Low interest rates, combined with few investment alternatives, left the Chinese consumer for years with little choice but to purchase residential real estate.

SHIFTS IN CONSUMER PREFERENCES. The COVID-19 pandemic changed the consuming, working, and leisure habits of tens of millions around the world. Some economic sectors benefited; others were negatively impacted. Some impacts were temporary; others are probably permanent.

Downtown office real estate, mass transit, and toll roads are some of the sectors that could be negatively impacted long term. These were built based on financial models that used occupancy, commuting, and ridership assumptions. Many of these assumptions need to be reviewed to the downside, and as revenues shrink, insolvencies will rise. In turn, this will have a ripple effect and impact many other sectors, starting with the lenders to such projects.

LAWS AND REGULATIONS. Governments may impact demand through legislation, regulation, and policies. Government mandates and incentives to shift to cleaner energy and electric vehicles are but two of the many examples where governments create demand for a given product and service. In the case of electric vehicles, the shift has affected demand in many sectors, from commodities, gas stations, and car dealerships to auto repairs. It may also have led to wasteful mistimed investments and subsidies as the early push for EV vehicles incorrectly assumed that the transition to EV vehicles would leapfrog over hybrid vehicles. Cannabis is another example of how legalization can create entire industries. Similarly, governments may suppress demand for products by banning their manufacture, importation, or distribution, including for environmental or safety reasons.

TECHNOLOGICAL DEVELOPMENTS. Changes in technology can come suddenly and be profound. The rate of change is accelerating and should continue to do so. In my lifetime, the world of music has gone from vinyl records that worked at various speeds, to cassettes, 8-tracks, CDs, MP3s, and finally streaming services. Some of these technologies lasted less than a decade. The same rapid change is true of many other consumer goods categories. Late-model mobile telephones and tablets have eviscerated demand for stand-alone cameras, video recorders, land-line telephones, recorders, radios, and alarm clocks, to name but a few affected areas.

NATURAL DISASTERS. Phrases like "global warming" and to a lesser extent "climate change" remain charged and often impede intelligent conversation about the cause and effect of natural disasters. Whatever the causes of such disasters, they are occurring with an increasing frequency and severity, with broad consequences. Insurers are revisiting risk and even refusing insurance coverage in certain areas and economic sectors. Agriculture is having to reduce water consumption and combat new parasites, desertification, wildfires, and other ills. Aside from threatening food security, climate change can force population migrations, thereby economically depressing whole areas while congesting others.

GEOPOLITICAL EVENTS. Wars, civil unrest, and sanctions are some of the unfortunate geopolitical events that can have wide ranging ripple effects. These events can disrupt demand through price increases resulting from scarcity. Ukraine is a major exporter of food, and the 2022 expansion of the Russian-Ukraine conflict has reduced food availability and increased prices in Global South countries.

SUPPLY

Supply risk designates the uncertainties posed by disruptions in the supply of inputs necessary for a project, including utilities and raw materials. A project requires a secure and uninterrupted supply of inputs upon reasonable terms and conditions. Project financiers will want to see long-term supply agreements from reliable providers for the more consequential or difficult-to-acquire project inputs. Factors that may impact supply are varied and may include:

SINGLE SOURCING. Many key inputs in the manufacture of products are made and sold by a handful of producers and sometimes, for patented inputs, one producer. Should such inputs not be readily available, then production will be affected. This is what occurred in 2020 and 2021 in the automotive sector when vehicle manufacturers around the world were confronted with widespread computer chip scarcity. There are very few advanced computer chip foundries in the world. During the early days of COVID-19, the foundries experienced disruptions and lower production. As a result, vehicle manufacturers had to ration and repurpose their limited supplies of chips. The manufacturers prioritized the production of higher-value vehicles, limited the number of extra features in vehicles, and temporarily stored vehicles until the missing chips became available. The pandemic caused so many bottlenecks and supply concerns that it singlehandedly forced car manufacturers to revisit their "just in time" (*kanban*) manufacturing and modify their inventories of parts and other supplies to ensure inventory buffers and avoid stock outs.

SUPPLIER LOCATION. Many commodities are sourced in countries that, for want of a better expression, are less than perfectly stable. There used to be a rule of thumb that each year, at least one government in Africa would experience a coup or insurrection. Companies that did business across Africa would include this assumption into their business plans and prepare accordingly. Unfortunately, in the early 2020s, the pace of disruption in Africa has accelerated and the assumption had to be revisited upward.

LOGISTICS. Congested infrastructure, shipping disruptions, and geopolitics are some of the events that may upend the timely delivery of inputs. The world's supply chains are full of potential bottlenecks, and it does not take much to cause serious interruptions, as demonstrated by the March 2021 blockage of the Suez Canal. The canal was blocked for six days when the four-hundred-metre-long *Ever Given* container ship ran aground because of high winds.

How a supply chain is structured may also exacerbate disruptions. As stated earlier, manufacturers used to keep large inventories of inputs to mitigate the effects of supply interruptions. Then, as logistics improved, manufacturers reduced their costs by reducing inventories on hand. It was a good move financially, but one that measurably increased the risk to their operations should a disruptive event occur.

TECHNOLOGY

Technology risk refers to the uncertainties arising from the use of technology and processes. Technology risk can stem from various sources, including:

UNPROVEN TECHNOLOGY. The maturity of a project's technology is very relevant. Generally, project financiers will only fund projects that use proven technology. They may accept innovations on the margins, but not in connection with an essential project element. Unproven technology increases the risk of failure, delays, cost overruns, and lower-than-anticipated production rates. Although technology risk is well understood, governments, large corporations, and wealthy entrepreneurs regularly fail to mitigate it. They often underestimate the risk and either have deep pockets and believe the issue may be resolved with money or they want to rush products to market to gain a competitive advantage.

A spectacular example of technology risk failure is the Olkiluoto 3 nuclear power plant in Finland. It was to be the first evolutionary power reactor (EPR) in the world. Construction started in 2005, and the plant was expected to be commissioned in 2009. The plant finally started commercial operation in 2023. The project was to be built for €3 billion. It is estimated to have costs of €11 billion, with the French contractor absorbing a loss equal to 50 percent of the final bill. The French government had to effectively rescue the contractor, one of France's global industrial champions. In addition to challenges caused by the novelty of the technology, the reports assessing the project's problems concluded that the contractor did not take into account the fact that the suppliers and subcontractors had not built a nuclear power plant since the 1980s, and many skills and much knowledge had been lost. In other words, the challenges of using an unproven technology were compounded by a lack of specialized construction know-how.

A recent example of the risk of rushing a product to market before its time was the lithium battery problem that plagued certain Samsung products in the mid-2010s. They were banned from flights in North America because of the risk of explosion and fire.

But perhaps nowhere is technology risk more prevalent than in the commercial satellite launch business, where about 5 percent of launches fail, sometimes spectacularly, each year.

SCALABILITY. The scalability of a technology is its ability to work at scale without material degradation as to performance. New technology may work in a laboratory or on a small scale, but fail at an industrial scale. This is a reason why pilot projects are used to further mitigate the risk. An example of technology that did not work well at scale was the retractable roof of the stadium purposefully built for the 1976 Montreal Olympic Games. The roof, completed in 1987, had two main elements: the world's tallest inclined tower at 165 metres and a 66 tonne, 5,500 m^2 Kevlar membrane. After the roof was commissioned more than ten years late, it quickly became evident that the roof was not fit for purpose. It could only be raised very slowly and never in winds above 40 km per hour. The innovative design had only been built twice at a much, much smaller scale in the more temperate French climate, in one case, over a public swimming pool outside of Paris. Moreover, both the tower and the membrane were plagued by construction and design problems. As a result, a permanent roof replaced the retractable one in 1998. That permanent roof is now plagued by problems and serious consideration is being given to replacing the roof once more at great cost, thus ensuring that the facility continues to gobble up precious financial resources. The Montreal Olympic stadium, at about C$4.1 billion on a 2024 inflation-adjusted basis, is one of the world's most expensive stadium ever built and, regrettably, has never delivered on its promise.

LAWS AND REGULATIONS. Laws, regulations, and policy may impact the suitability of technology. For example, many countries are reducing their carbon footprint, and certain fuels and processes will likely be proscribed in the medium to long term because they are not deemed part of the decarbonization climate solution. If a project has a twenty-five-year useful life, and uses a process that is likely to be challenged in the medium or even long term, the project is unlikely to be bankable.

OWNERSHIP. Technology risk may also arise if the ownership of a technology is unclear. This risk will only grow as more technology is developed through AI unless precautions are taken to ensure that third party proprietary knowledge is not improperly used. This is something that may be technically difficult to verify even with the best intentions.

PROJECT CONCEPTION

Project conception risk refers to the uncertainties from the moment an idea is conceived to the point where a project proposal is developed and approved for detailed planning and execution. This early phase is critical because it sets the foundation for the entire project. As mentioned previously in this book, there is an adage that the best way to mitigate project risks is to structure them out. This can be best done at the beginning, when the project is being conceived. Managing conception risk effectively is essential for successful project delivery. In the early stages of project conception, the objectives and goals of the project may not be well-defined or may change as stakeholders discuss and refine their ideas. At the end of the project conception process, the parameters of the project should have been settled and there should be little ambiguity as to the nature and scope of the project.

Project creep is one of the biggest risks to a project's scheduling, budget, commissioning, and performance. This risk is prevalent in large capital projects involving governments. These projects involve a lot of individuals and stakeholders, with each one desiring a say. The result is that projects can quickly become festooned with all sorts of non-essential bells and whistles and shrouded in much confusion as to the primary objective. I have experienced this in defence, mass transit, and bespoke software procurement. *The Pentagon Wars*, a 1998 HBO movie about the conceptual battles at the Pentagon over the development of the Bradley Fighting Vehicle, is a comedic illustration of the risk of having too many participants at the conception stage with the power to influence the scope of a project.

CONSTRUCTION

Construction risk refers to the uncertainties that can adversely impact the construction and commissioning of a project. Common construction risks include:

GEOTECHNICAL. This is the risk that site conditions, particularly below the surface, will impact the construction and cause delays and increased costs. Soil stability, inadequate site bearing capacity, groundwater, underground utilities and structures, and seismic activity are some of the geotechnical concerns that may affect construction. Soil characterization of the site is extremely important to mitigate the occurrence and consequences of geotechnical risk.

QUALITY. Quality issues are a major source of dispute. Defects or subpar quality can lead to rework and late project delivery, as well as adversely impact construction safety. There are many causes for poor quality: inadequate supervision, lack of know-how, and inferior materials, to name a few. But some of them may be cultural. I once asked a senior executive of a South Korean client whether he had noticed any differences between his country's approach to project conception and construction and that of Canada, where his company was building a sophisticated manufacturing facility. His response surprised me. He said that in Canada a lot of time was spent on project design and planning and that construction began only after that, while in South Korea construction started earlier and that detailed design and planning were often conducted in parallel with actual construction. Koreans just wanted to get on with it, even if it meant making mistakes and having to redo some of the work. He also added that he found construction prices in Canada, and particularly Quebec, to be relatively high, something others, including Continental Europeans have often mentioned to me. One cause often highlighted for the high prices in Quebec is the way the trades are classified, with Quebec having far more trade classifications than in other North American jurisdictions. Each trade, of course, has a monopoly on their on-site activities.

Construction is the source of much litigation and arbitration and has kept legions of lawyers and independent experts around the world busy and affluent. As a result, governments and some private owners prefer—when dealing with complex projects—to enter into sum-certain, date-certain engineering, procurement, and construction (EPC) contracts where nearly all the risks of the project construction and commissioning are passed on to the contractor. EPC contracts are more expensive, but they provide price certainty to the project owner. However, EPC contracts require contractors to have substantial resources and, as a result, may limit the pool of contractors that are able to bid for such projects.

OPERATIONS AND MAINTENANCE

Operations and maintenance risk is a broad category of risks that encompasses the potential for adverse failures within an organization's day-to-day operations. In some projects, the operations and/or maintenance of the project, once built and commissioned, is carried out by a third party. For example, the owner of a power plant may hire a third party, often called an O&M operator, to operate the plant and produce electricity. The risk here is that the O&M operator will fail to meet its obligations. If the cause of such failure is attributable to the O&M operator, then it will be liable for such failure. However, when the cause of the failure arises from a cause beyond the control of the O&M operator, the risk is borne by the party responsible for such cause. For example, the failure to meet certain construction specifications may adversely impact the operations of the project by increasing wear and tear and thus operating costs, in which case the construction contractor is responsible for such increased costs.

In some PPPs, the construction contractor and the O&M operator enter into an agreement with the owner that makes contractor and operator jointly and severally liable toward the owner for the proper operation and maintenance of the project. This agreement, often called an interface agreement, excludes the owner from any discussion between the contractor and the operator as to fault, leaving the contractor and operator to sort it out between themselves. In order to be effective, the interface agreement must delineate with care where the obligations of each of the contractor and the operator start and end.

SCHEDULING

The risk here is that an event will not occur or a milestone will not be reached on time. Most agreements recognize that certain scheduling failures are beyond the control of the parties and will provide relief. The consequences of scheduling risks will vary significantly depending on when the event occurs. Failures to meet a schedule early in a project will more often than not result in work reorganization or additional costs; however, failures that occur later in a project are generally more consequential, resulting not only in increased costs, but also in material delays that cause missed market opportunities and reduced profitability.

COST

This is the risk of non-budgeted increases in the construction, operation, and maintenance of a project. Such increases may be attributable to one or more parties in the project or a cause beyond their reasonable control:

POOR PLANNING. In my experience, the most common cause of cost overruns is poor planning and budgeting at project conception. In their eagerness to get on with a project or win a call for tenders or proposals, parties will often rush project preparation, only to get into financial trouble at a later stage. Poor planning leads to numerous change orders and rectifications. The more complex a project, the more planning it requires. Unfortunately, this rule of thumb is habitually ignored.

CONSTRUCTION. During construction, costs may rise from scope changes, supplier and contractor performance, material and labour availability, and permitting and licensing delays. To account for cost risk, project managers include contingency budgets in their plans; however, the adequacy of these contingencies is itself a source of risk and must be scrutinized carefully.

OPERATION. During operation, common risks of increased costs include poor project specifications, unproven technology and processes, latent defects, inflation, market fluctuations, and changes in laws and regulations.

ENVIRONMENT

Environmental risk is the risk that the project will adversely impact the environment. This risk has become a significant concern in recent decades due to a growing awareness of environmental issues and the importance of sustainability. The first time it became a topic of negotiation in a deal I was working on was in the late 1980s, when the subject matter of the transaction was a pulp and paper mill. When I first raised environment at the negotiating table, I was met with blank stares followed by strong language about tree huggers and time-wasters. Since I could get little information from the owner of the mill and, surprisingly, from the authorities, I dug up alarmist reports from Greenpeace, an international NGO, to provide a "factual" baseline and proceeded from that baseline, much to the chagrin of the other side. While much progress has been made on the environment thanks to advocacy groups, consumers, courts, and, interestingly, lenders and insurers cautious about being found responsible for pollution caused by borrowers, there is still much "greenwashing" and foot dragging on the subject.

PERMIT

Permitting risk is the risk that permits, authorizations, consents, clearances, and so on will not be issued or, more likely these days, will be issued only after lengthy delays and with a long list of conditions. This is particularly true in more economically developed jurisdictions. The private sector abhors delays and uncertainty. They increase costs. These can include increased interest expenses because capital is deployed for longer than budgeted. Inputs in large projects often require long lead times for design and manufacturing. And because project sponsors do not want to lose their place in the production cycle, it may be necessary to pay and take delivery of such inputs far in advance of the actual project timetable. In some cases, permitting delays may be so long as to allow for public sentiment to turn against a project, and imperilling it.

FORCE MAJEURE

"Force majeure" is a French phrase that refers to a civil law concept that excuses a failure to perform due to an irresistible and unforeseeable force. This concept has been borrowed by Anglo-American lawyers and expanded to contractually excuse non-performance by a party for causes that are clearly beyond the reasonable control of the affected party. In many negotiations, one of the parties will try to expand the ambit of the phrase while the other will try to limit it.

PARTICIPANT

Large, long-duration projects involve numerous participants. Participant risk is the risk that a participant is unable to perform their obligations. The cause of such inability may be:

FINANCIAL. The financial wherewithal of each project participant is very important. The lifeblood of any project is money. Without money, there can be no project activity. The risk here is that a project participant, such as a contractor, customer, financier, etc., will have insufficient funds when the time comes to perform their obligations.

TECHNICAL. Each participant must have the know-how and expertise required to carry out their obligations. As mentioned above, this was one of the major flaws with Olkiluoto 3. One "technical" risk often encountered in start-ups arises from the composition of the executive team. It has been my experience that if the team consists of individuals with little, if any, experience working together, the project is incurring a material, and potentially fatal, risk, notwithstanding the quality of each team member's CV.

LEGAL. A participant may be prevented from acting because of a change of law or regulation. For example, sanctions against a country may prevent a supplier from continuing to meet its obligations, such as when the US in April 2018 sanctioned UC Rusal, a Russian entity and one of the world's largest alumina and aluminum producer. The sanction obliged many aluminum smelters, including US producers, to scramble and seek alternate sources of alumina, failing which they would have to curtail or interrupt their production of aluminum or seek an exemption from the authorities.

FINANCING

Financing risk encompasses a wide range of financial challenges and uncertainties. Financing risk may render the project not bankable or prevent the renewal of its financing. Large, long-duration projects require sophisticated financing montages over long periods of time. The following are examples of financial risk:

REFINANCING RISK. A borrower may face difficulty refinancing loans or debt instruments on no less favourable terms if interest rates rise significantly or lending covenants are tightened.

CURRENCY EXCHANGE RISK. For international transactions, currency exchange fluctuations can impact the cost of goods, investments, and debt repayment.

INSURANCE

Insurance is the risk that some or all of the project's risks are not insurable, at least not on commercial terms. The inability to provide complete insurance coverage on commercial terms may impact the ability of the project to meet contractual, regulatory, or permitting requirements.

DOCUMENTATION

Most transactions, even relatively modest ones, are memorialized in more than one document. Large transactions require a large number of documents, sometimes hundreds. Documentation risk is the risk that the project's documentation does not adequately reflect all the elements of the transaction or that such elements are reflected in a contradictory manner. Project documentation often has different authors with varying styles.

Notwithstanding, it is essential to ensure that the documents dovetail properly with each other. This is easier said than done. One good place to start is to ensure that the documents use the same definitions; are coterminous and governed by the same laws, unless otherwise necessary; and provide uniform terms and conditions regarding breaches, remedies, and dispute resolution. Sometimes, the simplest action is to ensure that one agreement will cover those terms and conditions common to several agreements.

Specialized documentation (such as insurance policies, swap and derivative documentation, bank letters of credit, government decrees, licences, and permits) is usually negotiated and settled away from the main negotiation. It requires specialized knowledge to interpret and ensure that it dovetails with the main documentation.

RECORD KEEPING

Record keeping risk refers to the potential for negative consequences and operational disruptions to arise from inadequately managed or inaccurate documentation within an organization. Proper documentation is essential for efficient operations, compliance with laws and regulations, effective communication, and risk mitigation. Record keeping risk can have many causes, including incomplete or outdated information, data-entry errors, failure to comply with laws and regulations, inefficient document retrieval, confidentiality breaches, and ineffective document and data retention. Poor record keeping can also hinder business continuity, resulting in project creep or drift and in the loss of institutional memory.

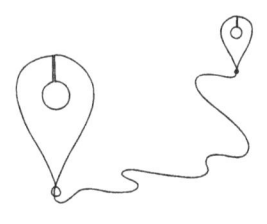

APPENDIX II

NON-COMMERCIAL RISKS

The phrase "non-commercial risks" generally refers to risks that do not stem from the project. Non-commercial risks include political, macroeconomic, and legal risks. There is a view among some investors that non-commercial risks arise primarily in lesser-developed countries. This is definitively not my experience. On the contrary, political and other non-commercial risks are present in all jurisdictions, but tend to be somewhat more subtle in more economically advanced jurisdictions.

The following is a brief listing of the more common non-commercial risks:

ARMED CONFLICTS

Risks involving armed conflicts refer to the uncertainties stemming from armed conflict in all its forms, between states and between states and non-state actors, and how such conflicts may directly or indirectly impact a project.

According to the Geneva Academy of International Humanitarian Law and Human Rights, there were well over one hundred conflicts of all types around the world in 2023 with the potential for new ones to be continuously added to the list. One possible new conflict involves Essequibo. In 2023, Venezuela resurrected its ownership claim to the Essequibo region in neighbouring Guyana. The contested region represents approximately two-thirds of the territory of Guyana. Important oil discoveries were made by Exxon Mobil in 2015 off the coast of Essequibo and Guyana has since issued production licences to Exxon Mobil.

These oil deposits have made Guyana's territorial waters very valuable. In early 2024, Exxon Mobil announced that it was pumping about 645,000 barrels a day from offshore oilfields. Venezuela, a country with a woefully mismanaged economy, took the opportunity in 2023 to distract from its poor performance at home by focusing on Essequibo. To increase its negotiating leverage, Venezuela held a consultative referendum on December 3, 2023, regarding its territorial claim and future actions. There were five questions dealing with the matter, and all were overwhelmingly answered in favour of the government. Some referendum questions opened the door to military action. Although both countries have agreed to peacefully resolve the dispute, there is always the danger that the matter could escalate militarily and involve others. Shortly after Venezuela announced its renewed claim on Essequibo, and the holding of a referendum, the US and UK navies dispatched vessels to the area to show the flag and dissuade provocation.

NATIONAL SECURITY

National security risk refers to a state invoking national security to interfere with business activities, including the purchase and sale of businesses, foreign direct investment, or the import or export of products and services. Some countries, including the US and China, broadly define what constitutes national security and often invoke it to justify actions taken across a wide array of matters that in most other jurisdictions would not be raised to such a level of concern. National security risk can come in many different shapes, including:

MILITARILY. This is the risk that a state may not be able to dissuade or thwart an aggressor from military action against it.

POLITICAL. This is the risk posed by threats to state institutions by domestic and foreign actors. It can take various forms, including propaganda, disinformation, election interference, corruption, political violence, terrorism, and widespread civil unrest.

ECONOMICAL. This is the risk that the economic stability and prosperity of a country will be challenged by another state, whether fairly or unfairly. The competitive advantage of a nation may change quickly as a result of technological change, the discovery of new mineral wealth, or geopolitical events elsewhere, including in foreign markets. The US fears the economic and military rise of China and regularly invokes national security to impose exports and import controls and other measures against China.

ENVIRONMENTAL. This is the risk that environmental change, whether gradual or abrupt, will adversely impact a nation. Droughts and storms, for example, can cause countries to reduce exports of food at times of poor harvest.

LEGAL AND REGULATORY

Investors want to know the legal framework applicable to their project, including how laws and regulations are interpreted, enforced, and modified. My experience is that investors want to know the "rules of the road" early on and have a marked preference for limited changes to such rules during the life of the investment.

In the Chad pipeline file, one of our first tasks was to determine the applicable law. The country was recovering from a lengthy civil war, and we needed to answer the questions "Is there law?" and, if so, "What is it?" During French colonial times, Chad was considered a backwater of inferior economic value. Its legal system was essentially a hodgepodge of laws adopted in other French colonies. The French often did not even make the effort to print some laws applicable to Chad, preferring simply to stamp the laws of other colonies with words indicating that they also applied to the Chad colony. Our task was to identify the body of pre-independence laws and determine which ones continued to have currency. A similar exercise, albeit somewhat easier, was also conducted for the post-independence period.

A decade later, in Vietnam, we were confronted with the reverse situation. Various levels of governments were gleefully adopting laws and regulations, often dealing with the same subject, all without a centralized repertory or system for publicizing them. To make matters worse, it was not always clear which law prevailed in the case of conflicting provisions. The resulting legal and regulatory confusion materially delayed our client's project and took considerable time and effort to clear up.

EXTRA-TERRITORIAL APPLICATION OF LAWS

This is the risk that a nation with *no* direct link to a project will adopt a law or regulation or apply its laws or regulations in a manner that adversely affects the project. The US is probably the jurisdiction that poses the greatest extra-territorial legal risk. Thanks to the size of its economy, and the preponderant use of the US dollar in international trade, the US asserts partial jurisdiction over much of the world's trade. The growing use of unilateral sanctions by the US against countries, businesses, and individuals means that the risk of either running afoul of US laws and regulations or being adversely affected by them must be carefully considered when structuring projects, even when the project has no manifest link to the US.

The Meng Wanzhou/Huawei saga is an example of the very broad reach given by the US to its laws and regulations and the Kafkaesque consequences that may ensue from such reach. Huawei Technologies (Huawei) is a Chinese manufacturer of advanced telephone equipment. The company sells equipment all over the world. Huawei and its founder, Ren Zhengfei, are closely associated with the higher echelons of the Chinese government. The US and many of its close allies have banned the use of Huawei equipment in their telephone infrastructure as a precaution against China spying, or otherwise interfering with their telecommunications infrastructure.

In August 2018, a judge in New York City issued an arrest warrant for Meng Wanzhou, a Chinese citizen — and daughter of Huawei's founder — who at the time was the CFO of Huawei. The stated rationale for US action was that the US wanted to protect a financial institution from running afoul of US laws, namely sanctions against doing business with Iran. China viewed the US arrest warrant as a politically motivated attempt by the US to inflict damage on Huawei, one of China's most successful companies.

On December 1, 2018, Wanzhou was arrested in Vancouver by the Royal Canadian Mounted Police acting at the request of US authorities under the terms of the Canada-US extradition treaty. Wanzhou was travelling for business from Hong Kong to Mexico and was only making a brief stopover in Vancouver. The arrest placed Canada in an unenviable position between two superpowers, one being Canada's neighbour, military protector, and number one trading partner. The US firmly expected Canada to fulfill its treaty obligations. Meanwhile, China, an important trading partner, demanded that Canada forthwith release Wanzhou and let her continue her journey.

On December 10, 2018, two Canadians, Michael Kovrig and Michael Spavor, were arrested and incarcerated in China on espionage charges. They would become known as the "Two Michaels." Canada objected to the arrests, demanded that China cease and desist from "hostage diplomacy" and that the Two Michaels be released forthwith. China denied any linkage with the Wanzhou arrest. On December 11, 2018, Wanzhou was released on bail but placed under house arrest in her comfortable Vancouver home.

On January 19, 2019, the US issued its formal extradition request and listed several counts of bank fraud, wire fraud, and conspiracies to commit bank and wire fraud in relation to financial transactions involving Iran. The charges only had a remote factual connection with the US and required some mental gymnastics to arrive at the conclusions of the US authorities.

Wanzhou and her lawyers vigorously challenged the extradition request. In August 2021, the Canadian judge reviewing the US extradition request openly questioned the factual and legal basis for the US request and queried whether the facts were sufficient to extradite Wanzhou.

On September 24, 2021, after a conversation between the leaders of China and the US, the US announced that it had reached a deferred prosecution agreement with Wanzhou. Wanzhou was released from house arrest on that day and immediately flew to China. On the same day, the Two Michaels were released after more than one thousand miserable days in prison and immediately returned to Canada.

On December 2, 2022, a US judge dismissed the charges against Wanzhou in accordance with the deferred prosecution agreement.

The above example—begun under President Trump and settled under the Biden administration—illustrates the great lengths the US sometimes goes to apply pressure in furtherance of its geopolitical goals, and the unfortunate consequences such actions may have.

The cumulative effect of US sanctions and other legal actions is adversely affecting that country's standing in the world and may, in the medium term, threaten its ability to finance itself by selling debt to foreign investors. The US benefits greatly from the US dollar being the world's primary reserve currency, but many countries, including China, Russia, India, and Brazil, are actively seeking alternatives. Moreover, sanction fatigue is increasing with many countries publicly saying they will not enforce unilateral US sanctions or actions taken in furtherance of such sanctions.

The US dollar is not about to lose its preponderance in world trade, but the increasing weaponization of the US dollar is corrosive to its continued use as a reserve currency. A reserve currency should be neutral and sanctions involving its use applied very sparingly and as a result of a broad consensus.

EXPROPRIATION

Expropriation risk is the risk that the project will be expropriated or nationalized. Investors will not embark on a project and devote time and capital to it if there is a credible chance that their project will be taken from them in the foreseeable future. Most legal systems and bilateral and multilateral foreign investment protection treaties recognize the right of a government to expropriate private property for certain purposes, provided fair compensation is paid.

Some governmental actions may have the same effect as an outright expropriation. For example, the refusal by a government to deliver or renew an essential permit may amount to an expropriation by other means. This is often the case in long-gestation projects when changes in government or public sentiment causes a government not to grant an essential authorizations.

The danger here for the investor is that it may not be entitled to compensation under local laws. In other words, the risk of government action, or inaction in these instances, is allocated to the project sponsors. In such cases, mitigation strategies for foreign investors include buying political risk insurance, structuring the project to benefit from investor protection under investment treaties, or, perhaps less advantageously, obtaining written assurances from the authorities at the outset of the project and specifying the consequences for any breach.

CURRENCY

Currency risk is the risk posed on the free flow of money. Restrictions may manifest themselves in a variety of ways, such as restrictions on the convertibility of local currency, the inability to remit funds abroad or pay foreign creditors, or the obligation to maintain substantial deposits in local currency at local banks. The impediment may be legal, or it may be caused by macroeconomic factors. For example, the banks in a country may have insufficient hard currency on hand to meet exchange requests. The mitigation strategies for foreign investors include buying political risk insurance and, if the production of the project is exported and paid in hard currency, structuring the project so that all sale proceeds are first remitted to the project's offshore accounts. Thereafter, only the funds required to pay local costs and taxes are transferred into the country.

CYBERCRIME

Cybercrime is the risk posed by hackers entering a project's IT network and stealing money and data from it or disabling or freezing the IT network, whether for ransom or other motive.

TRADE SANCTIONS

This is the risk posed by one trading bloc or country imposing trade constraints. These may include export and import bans, high custom tariffs, stringent product specifications, and other so-called, non-tariff barriers. The US and the European Union are great users of trade constraints. They represent more than half of the world's household consumption expenditures and, as a result, have clout. But high government and consumer debt levels in the US and the European Union, and lower usage of the US dollar in international transactions and as a reserve currency, could gradually cause the effectiveness of US and European Union trade sanctions to wane.

MACROECONOMIC RISK

Macroeconomic risk is the risk posed by general economic conditions in a relevant jurisdiction, whether in the project's host jurisdiction or in a principal market for the project's output. This risk includes interest rate increases, currency fluctuations and devaluations, taxation, and government debt default.

CLIMATE

Climate risk is the risk that the project is, directly or indirectly, negatively impacted by climate events — such as cyclones, flooding, tsunamis, earthquakes, droughts, and forest fires — and is unable to recover rapidly.

INSTITUTIONAL CAPACITY

Institutional capacity is the risk that the civil service of a country does not have the skills and incentives to operate at the required level. Many countries, often with the assistance of IFIs and bilateral aid agencies, have adopted laws and regulations that are complex and well beyond the institutional capacity of the civil service. As a result, these laws are often misinterpreted, poorly enforced, and honoured in the breach. They can also serve as opportunities for corrupt behaviour.

CORRUPTION

Corruption risk is the risk that corruption, collusion, and other unlawful restraints of trade practices will have a material impact on competition for a project or on the costs and output of such project. Corruption—notwithstanding the many public statements and initiatives against it around the world—continues to be a "business" worth hundreds of billion dollars a year. SOEs and construction and extractive industries, such as mining and oil and gas, are particularly susceptible to corruption and other nefarious practices.

Corruption, collusion, and other such behaviour are not victimless crimes. They increase prices and affect quality and performance. These practices are effectively a tax borne by the collectivity, often disproportionately by the poor and most vulnerable. These crimes are difficult to detect, and few countries attempt to do so with conviction and means. This is even truer when the crimes are committed abroad. Countries that do the most to combat foreign corruption practices do so primarily out of self-interest.

Because of its financial, diplomatic, and military reach, the US is probably the most effective at combatting foreign corruption when it decides to do so.

I arrived in Japan during the Lockheed bribery scandals. Lockheed, a US aerospace company and maker of military and civilian aircraft, was being investigated by the US for having given bribes to very high officials in the Netherlands, Italy, West Germany, and Japan in connection with the sale of its aircrafts. In Japan, the scandal ensnared scores of politicians, businessmen, and others, including underworld figures and even a priest. Headlines dealing with the scandal were constant. The scandal involved former prime minister Kakuei Tanaka, one of Japan's most powerful postwar politicians. Tanaka was convicted in 1983 of having contravened Japan's foreign exchange law. He was not convicted of bribery. He was given a prison sentence, but appealed it. The Japanese judiciary, which moves at a very deliberate pace in usual times, was slowed down even further to allow Tanaka to remain free until his death in 1993.

At the start of my career, corruption in international transactions was reluctantly viewed as an unfortunate but necessary practice, with some jurisdictions even allowing bribes to be deducted for tax purposes as business expenses. Nowadays corruption results in severe consequences for those individuals and businesses involved if, and it is a big if, the bad behaviour is detected, investigated, and successfully prosecuted. There is still much work to do to combat corruption and other bad practices, but at least it is no longer viewed as "normal" behaviour by much of the world.

Corruption is often organized and involves many individuals across several sectors. This makes it more difficult to repress, particularly where there is a lack of transparency. Corruption, and other bad behaviour, thrives in the shadows, and it is no coincidence that one of the best-known anti-corruption organizations is called Transparency International.

I have, from time to time, raised the subject of corruption with clients, both public and private, and I remain amazed by the range of emotions and attitudes I have encountered. They go from denial, incredulity, annoyance, rationalization, and, more recently, promises of investigation that are often quickly forgotten. But the one reaction that puzzled me the most was feigned disinterest. I remember organizing a conference on corruption in Montreal in the 2010s. It was announced well in advance, and the conference was ostensibly about the corruption of foreign civil servants so as not to ruffle any local feathers. Interest was so low that I had to cancel the conference.

The next year, after a large corruption scandal in Quebec was uncovered and making headlines, I again organized the same conference. It was sold out within days, with many interested persons turned away. After the conference, it dawned on me that the audience was not disinterested but rather afraid of being tainted by the subject matter. In other words, participation in these types of conferences could be interpreted as admission that something was amiss within their organizations. The scandal in Quebec and the accompanying media coverage had given cover for participants to openly participate with little fear of reputation risk.

REPUTATION

Reputation risk is the potential for public perception to negatively impact a project or a project participant. Reputation risk can arise from numerous causes and have serious consequences. A government's poor reputation as an investor-friendly jurisdiction may result in prospective investors shunning that jurisdiction. A corporation's less-than-stellar reputation may cause employees to leave, suppliers to sever business ties, financiers to refuse to finance, and consumers to boycott the corporation's products and services.

Reputation risk may also cause a corporation to leave a jurisdiction or divest itself from an investment. A good divestment case study is how Talisman Energy, a Canadian oil producer, was pressured to sell its minority participation in Greater Nile Petroleum Operating Company (GNOC). GNOC had oil production activities in the state of Kordofan in the western part of Sudan. As the political and military situation in Darfur and Kordofan worsened in the early '00s, Talisman came under sustained and blistering governmental and civil society criticism regarding its investment in GNOC. After putting up much resistance, Talisman finally sold its participation to the China Petroleum Corporation in 2003.

GLOSSARY OF ABBREVIATIONS

ADB: Asian Development Bank

AI: artificial intelligence

AMR: Anderson Mōri & Rabinowitz

CCPT: Courtois, Clarkson, Parsons, and Tétrault

EGAT: Electricity Generating Authority of Thailand

FLA: foreign legal apprentice

HQ: Hydro-Québec

IFC: International Finance Corporation

IFI: international financial institution

IMF: International Monetary Fund

IPO: initial public offering

IPP: independent power producer

OECD: the Organisation for Economic Co-Operation and Development

PPP: public-private partnership

TSE: Toronto Stock Exchange

SE: Stikeman Elliott LLP

SEB: state electricity board

SOE: state-owned enterprise

WTO: World Trade Organization

www.ingramcontent.com/pod-product-compliance
Lightning Source LLC
Chambersburg PA
CBHW020249120125
20249CB00009B/268